# the hummingbird bakery
## cookbook

Tarek Malouf and The Hummingbird Bakers

photography by Peter Cassidy

RYLAND
PETERS
& SMALL

LONDON  NEW YORK

**Design, Photographic Art Direction and Prop Styling** Steve Painter
**Senior Editor** Céline Hughes
**Production Manager** Patricia Harrington
**Art Director** Leslie Harrington
**Publishing Director** Alison Starling

**Food Stylist** Bridget Sargeson
**Indexer** Hilary Bird

**Hummingbird Bakery corporate branding and company graphic design** Sue Thedens
**Illustrations** Debbie Adamson

First published in the UK in 2009
by Ryland Peters & Small
20-21 Jockey's Fields
London WC1R 4BW
www.rylandpeters.com

10 9 8 7 6 5 4 3

Text © Tarek Malouf and The Hummingbird Bakery 2009
Design and photographs
© Ryland Peters & Small 2009

Printed in China

The author's moral rights have been asserted. All rights reserved. No part of this publication may be reproduced, stored in a retrieval system, or transmitted in any form or by any means, electronic, mechanical, photocopying, or otherwise, without the prior permission of the publisher.

ISBN: 978 1 84597 830 3

A CIP record for this book is available from the British Library.

**Notes**
- The cupcakes on pages 14–45 were baked in American-style cupcake cases, which are larger than standard UK cases. If using standard cases, the yield will be approximately 18 instead of 12. They will need 3–5 minutes less in the oven.
- All spoon measurements are level, unless otherwise specified.
- All eggs are medium, unless otherwise specified. It is generally recommended that free-range eggs be used. Uncooked or partially cooked eggs should not be served to the very young, the very old, those with compromised immune systems, or to pregnant women.
- Ovens should be preheated to the specified temperature. Recipes in this book were tested using a regular oven. If using a fan-assisted oven, follow the manufacturer's instructions for adjusting temperatures.

## contents

- 6 welcome to the hummingbird bakery
- 12 cupcakes
- 46 cakes
- 78 pies
- 98 brownies and bars
- 114 muffins
- 128 cookies
- 142 index
- 144 acknowledgements

# Welcome to The Hummingbird Bakery

I first thought about opening The Hummingbird Bakery after spending Thanksgiving with cousins in North Carolina. After eating too much pecan pie, banana cream pie and apple pie, I wondered why there wasn't a place in London that made these types of desserts to a high standard. On subsequent trips to the USA, and New York in particular, I visited various bakeries that made all the goodies that I enjoyed eating, especially cupcakes. At that point, cupcakes seemed to be unknown in London – at least, they were hard to buy.

I started planning the Bakery in 2002. First, I attended baking classes in New York so that I would understand the ingredients and techniques used in American baking. Then came the fun task of devising recipes and testing them on friends and family. I always had an idea of which core cakes I wanted to sell – and for these I tested and tweaked many, many recipes until I found what I thought tasted the most authentic. I even held parties for friends so that they could test the recipes and tell me if I was getting them right.

The next important step was finding the perfect site for the first shop. I felt it should be a place that was relatively busy, with a bohemian feel. A unit in Portobello Road in London's Notting Hill came up by chance and I immediately jumped on it. It proved to be heaven-sent because as soon as the shop opened, a lot of high-profile customers began to write and speak about it. On Saturdays, when the famous market is on, tourists flock to Portobello and they were soon queueing up to try our cupcakes. During the quieter weekdays, the publicity surrounding the Bakery kept it busy. Soon, recommendations were appearing on blogs, and friends were being urged to try our cupcakes when they visited London. Now, thanks to the success of our first branch, we also have a shop in South Kensington.

It will probably come as no surprise that we sell far more cupcakes than anything else. They seem to be popular because of their cute size, the childhood memories they evoke and their sheer versatility. Our best-selling cupcakes are vanilla with pink frosting, which reflects our female-dominated customer base, and red velvet, simply because they look and taste so distinctive. For many people, layer-cakes are essential for birthdays. Besides the red velvet and vanilla, our carrot cake is extremely popular. Decorating a three-layered cake takes time but the result is worth the effort! Pies are such an American tradition, especially for festive occasions. Our customers love lemon meringue and key lime pies the most – the fluffy meringue and whipped cream toppings are so beautiful and mouth-watering that they never last long in the shop. Other treats such as muffins, cookies and bars were always favourites in school lunchboxes when I was at school. Our brownies are extremely popular, so we developed three versions: plain (no nuts), frosted (more cakey with nuts and frosting) and my favourite, brownies topped with baked cheesecake and raspberry whipped cream!

I'm so pleased to share my favourite cakes and bakes with you in this book. I hope you enjoy baking them as much we all do at The Hummingbird Bakery.

Tarek Malouf

# frostings

These frostings make enough to frost 12 cupcakes. To cover a cake (top and sides), double the recipes. They are used in cupcake and cake recipes throughout the book. Dye the Vanilla or Cream Cheese frostings any shade you like with a couple of drops of food colouring mixed in until evenly incorporated. At the Hummingbird, we like our cupcake frostings in pretty candy colours, but you can choose any colour you like.

## vanilla

250 g icing sugar, sifted
80 g unsalted butter, at room temperature
25 ml whole milk
a couple of drops of vanilla extract

**Makes enough to frost 12 cupcakes (double the recipe for 20-cm cake)**

Beat the icing sugar and butter together in a freestanding electric mixer with a paddle attachment (or use a handheld electric whisk) on medium-slow speed until the mixture comes together and is well mixed. Turn the mixer down to slow speed. Combine the milk and vanilla extract in a separate bowl, then add to the butter mixture a couple of tablespoons at a time. Once all the milk has been incorporated, turn the mixer up to high speed. Continue beating until the frosting is light and fluffy, at least 5 minutes. The longer the frosting is beaten, the fluffier and lighter it becomes.

## chocolate

300 g icing sugar, sifted
100 g unsalted butter, at room temperature
40 g cocoa powder, sifted
40 ml whole milk

**Makes enough to frost 12 cupcakes (double the recipe for 20-cm cake)**

Beat the icing sugar, butter and cocoa powder together in a freestanding electric mixer with a paddle attachment (or use a handheld electric whisk) on medium-slow speed until the mixture comes together and is well mixed. Turn the mixer down to slow speed. Add the milk to the butter mixture a couple of tablespoons at a time. Once all the milk has been incorporated, turn the mixer up to high speed. Continue beating until the frosting is light and fluffy, about 5 minutes. The longer the frosting is beaten, the fluffier and lighter it becomes.

## cream cheese

300 g icing sugar, sifted
50 g unsalted butter, at room temperature
125 g cream cheese, cold

**Makes enough to frost 12 cupcakes (double the recipe for 20-cm cake)**

Beat the icing sugar and butter together in a freestanding electric mixer with a paddle attachment (or use a handheld electric whisk) on medium-slow speed until the mixture comes together and is well mixed. Add the cream cheese in one go and beat until it is completely incorporated. Turn the mixer up to medium-high speed. Continue beating until the frosting is light and fluffy, at least 5 minutes. Do not overbeat, as it can quickly become runny.

# cupcakes

# vanilla cupcakes

Our vanilla cupcakes, topped with candy-coloured Vanilla Frosting and sprinkles, are what the Hummingbird Bakery is best known for, and they never fail to please. When you make these at home, don't overcook them – they should be light golden and spring back when touched. This way you will ensure an airy, moist sponge with a subtle vanilla taste. The cupcakes can also be topped with Chocolate Frosting (see page 11).

120 g plain flour
140 g caster sugar
1½ teaspoons baking powder
a pinch of salt
40 g unsalted butter, at room temperature
120 ml whole milk
1 egg
¼ teaspoon vanilla extract
1 quantity Vanilla Frosting (page 11)
hundreds and thousands or other edible sprinkles, to decorate

*a 12-hole cupcake tray, lined with paper cases (see note on page 4)*

**Makes 12**

Preheat the oven to 170°C (325°F) Gas 3.

Put the flour, sugar, baking powder, salt and butter in a freestanding electric mixer with a paddle attachment (or use a handheld electric whisk) and beat on slow speed until you get a sandy consistency and everything is combined. Gradually pour in half the milk and beat until the milk is just incorporated.

Whisk the egg, vanilla extract and remaining milk together in a separate bowl for a few seconds, then pour into the flour mixture and continue beating until just incorporated (scrape any unmixed ingredients from the side of the bowl with a rubber spatula). Continue mixing for a couple more minutes until the mixture is smooth. Do not overmix.

Spoon the mixture into the paper cases until two-thirds full and bake in the preheated oven for 20–25 minutes, or until light golden and the sponge bounces back when touched. A skewer inserted in the centre should come out clean. Leave the cupcakes to cool slightly in the tray before turning out onto a wire cooling rack to cool completely.

When the cupcakes are cold, spoon the Vanilla Frosting on top and decorate with hundreds and thousands.

# chocolate cupcakes

We use a devil's food cake for our chocolate base. The cocoa powder gives the sponge a dark colour and chocolatey kick. The sponge should be light and moist, with all the ingredients well incorporated. But don't overbeat the mixture, as the sponge will be too heavy. For chocolate lovers, top with Chocolate Frosting (see page 11). For a more restrained option, both the Vanilla and Cream Cheese Frostings work well.

100 g plain flour

20 g cocoa powder

140 g caster sugar

1½ teaspoons baking powder

a pinch of salt

40 g unsalted butter, at room temperature

120 ml whole milk

1 egg

¼ teaspoon vanilla extract

1 quantity Chocolate, Vanilla or Cream Cheese Frosting (page 11)

chocolate vermicelli or edible silver balls, to decorate

*a 12-hole cupcake tray, lined with paper cases (see note on page 4)*

**Makes 12**

Preheat the oven to 170°C (325°F) Gas 3.

Put the flour, cocoa powder, sugar, baking powder, salt and butter in a freestanding electric mixer with a paddle attachment (or use a handheld electric whisk) and beat on slow speed until you get a sandy consistency and everything is combined.

Whisk the milk, egg and vanilla extract together in a jug, then slowly pour about half into the flour mixture, beat to combine and turn the mixer up to high speed to get rid of any lumps.

Turn the mixer down to a slower speed and slowly pour in the remaining milk mixture (scrape any unmixed ingredients from the side of the bowl with a rubber spatula). Continue mixing for a couple more minutes until the mixture is smooth. Do not overmix.

Spoon the mixture into the paper cases until two-thirds full and bake in the preheated oven for 20–25 minutes, or until the sponge bounces back when touched. A skewer inserted in the centre should come out clean. Leave the cupcakes to cool slightly in the tray before turning out onto a wire cooling rack to cool completely.

When the cupcakes are cold, spoon the Chocolate, Vanilla or Cream Cheese Frosting on top and decorate with chocolate vermicelli or silver balls.

# red velvet cupcakes

It seems people can't resist the red velvet cupcakes' deep red sponge with white Cream Cheese Frosting. Mix all the ingredients well so that the sponge has an even colour and texture. For added colour contrast, you can crumble some extra red velvet sponge over the cupcakes. To make a red velvet cake instead, double the quantities below, divide between three 20-cm cake tins and bake for 25 minutes at the same oven temperature. Frost with 2 quantities of Cream Cheese Frosting.

60 g unsalted butter, at room temperature

150 g caster sugar

1 egg

20 g cocoa powder

40 ml red food colouring

½ teaspoon vanilla extract

120 ml buttermilk

150 g plain flour

½ teaspoon bicarbonate of soda

1½ teaspoons white vinegar

1 quantity Cream Cheese Frosting (page 11)

*a 12-hole cupcake tray, lined with paper cases (see note on page 4)*

**Makes 12**

Preheat the oven to 170°C (325°F) Gas 3.

Put the butter and the sugar in a freestanding electric mixer with a paddle attachment (or use a handheld electric whisk) and beat on medium speed until light and fluffy and well mixed. Turn the mixer up to high speed, slowly add the egg and beat until everything is well incorporated.

In a separate bowl, mix together the cocoa powder, red food colouring and vanilla extract to make a very thick, dark paste. Add to the butter mixture and mix thoroughly until evenly combined and coloured (scrape any unmixed ingredients from the side of the bowl with a rubber spatula). Turn the mixer down to slow speed and slowly pour in half the buttermilk. Beat until well mixed, then add half the flour and beat until everything is well incorporated. Repeat this process until all the buttermilk and flour have been added. Scrape down the side of the bowl again. Turn the mixer up to high speed and beat until you have a smooth, even mixture. Turn the mixer down to low speed and add the bicarbonate of soda and vinegar. Beat until well mixed, then turn up the speed again and beat for a couple more minutes.

Spoon the mixture into the paper cases until two-thirds full and bake in the preheated oven for 20–25 minutes, or until the sponge bounces back when touched. A skewer inserted in the centre should come out clean. Leave the cupcakes to cool slightly in the tray before turning out onto a wire cooling rack to cool completely.

When the cupcakes are cold, spoon the Cream Cheese Frosting on top.

**See photographs on pages 18 and 19.**

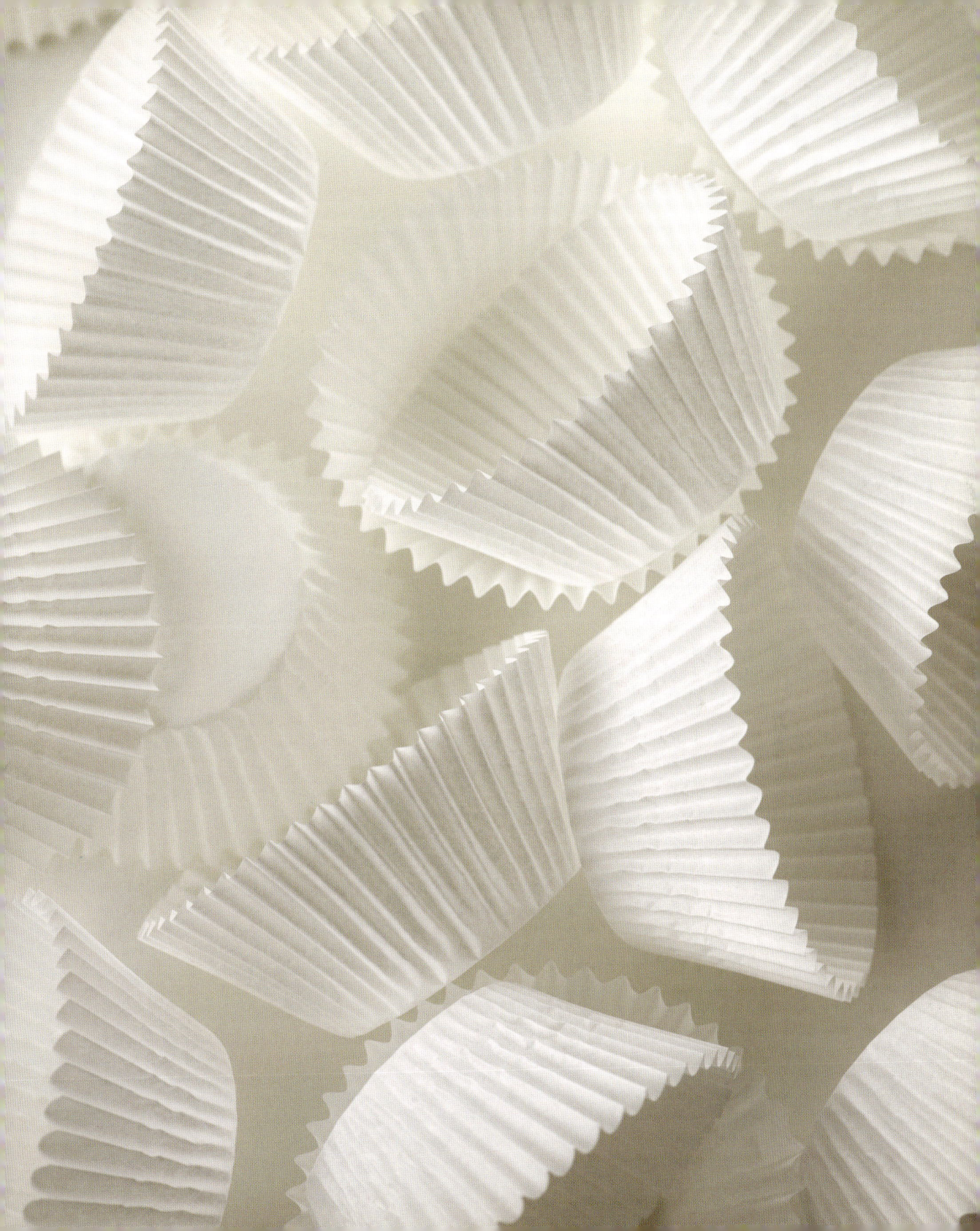

# lemon cupcakes

**Hollowing out a bit of the sponge and putting in a small spoonful of lemon curd makes this cupcake very moist and tangy. Lemon is always a popular alternative to chocolate or vanilla desserts. The trick is to keep the frosting slightly tart, to temper the sugar.**

120 g plain flour

150 g caster sugar

1½ teaspoons baking powder

2 tablespoons grated lemon zest, plus extra to decorate

40 g unsalted butter, at room temperature

120 ml whole milk

1 egg

**lemon frosting**

250 g icing sugar, sifted

80 g unsalted butter, at room temperature

2 tablespoons grated lemon zest

a couple of drops of yellow food colouring (optional)

25 ml whole milk

*a 12-hole cupcake tray, lined with paper cases (see note on page 4)*

**Makes 12**

Preheat the oven to 170°C (325°F) Gas 3.

Put the flour, sugar, baking powder, lemon zest and butter in a freestanding electric mixer with a paddle attachment (or use a handheld electric whisk) and beat on slow speed until you get a sandy consistency and everything is combined. Gradually pour in the milk and beat until just incorporated.

Add the egg to the flour mixture and continue beating until just incorporated (scrape any unmixed ingredients from the side of the bowl with a rubber spatula). Continue mixing for a couple more minutes until the mixture is smooth. Do not overmix.

Spoon the mixture into the paper cases until two-thirds full and bake in the preheated oven for 20–25 minutes, or until the sponge bounces back when touched. A skewer inserted in the centre should come out clean. Leave the cupcakes to cool slightly in the tray before turning out onto a wire cooling rack to cool completely.

**For the lemon frosting:** Beat together the icing sugar, butter, lemon zest and food colouring, if using, in a freestanding electric mixer with a paddle attachment (or use a handheld electric whisk) on medium-slow speed until the mixture comes together and is well mixed. Turn the mixer down to a slower speed. Slowly pour in the milk, then when it is all incorporated, turn the mixer up to high speed. Continue beating until the frosting is light and fluffy, at least 5 minutes. The longer the frosting is beaten, the fluffier and lighter it becomes.

When the cupcakes are cold, spoon the lemon frosting on top and decorate with a little lemon zest.

# strawberry cheesecake cupcakes

It's important to use pieces of fresh strawberry in this recipe – they moisten the sponge and texture of the cupcakes. The crumbled digestive biscuits sprinkled on top add the flavour of a cheesecake base.

120 g plain flour
140 g caster sugar
1½ teaspoons baking powder
a pinch of salt
40 g unsalted butter, at room temperature
120 ml whole milk
½ teaspoon vanilla extract
1 egg
12 large strawberries, chopped into small pieces
200 g digestive biscuits
1 quantity Cream Cheese Frosting (page 11)

*a 12-hole cupcake tray, lined with paper cases (see note on page 4)*

**Makes 12**

Preheat the oven to 170°C (325°F) Gas 3.

Put the flour, sugar, baking powder, salt and butter in a freestanding electric mixer with a paddle attachment (or use a handheld electric whisk) and beat on slow speed until you get a sandy consistency and everything is combined.

Pour in the milk and vanilla extract and beat on medium speed until all the ingredients are well mixed (scrape any unmixed ingredients from the side of the bowl with a rubber spatula). Add the egg and beat well for a few minutes to ensure the ingredients are well incorporated.

Divide the chopped strawberries between the paper cases. Spoon the cupcake mixture on top until two-thirds full and bake in the preheated oven for 20–25 minutes, or until light golden and the sponge bounces back when touched. A skewer inserted in the centre should come out clean. Leave the cupcakes to cool slightly in the tray before turning out onto a wire cooling rack to cool completely.

Roughly break up the digestive biscuits and put them in a food processor. Process until finely ground. When the cupcakes are cold, spoon the Cream Cheese Frosting on top and finish with a sprinkling of finely ground biscuits.

# black bottom cupcakes

The black bottom cupcake looks innocent, but packs a punch! A dark chocolate sponge with a dollop of cheesecake baked into it, we top ours with Cream Cheese Frosting for extra impact. The chocolate sponge base is different from our normal chocolate cupcakes – it's darker, slightly less sweet and marries well with the cheesecake centre. Omit the cream cheese frosting for a more moderate treat.

1 quantity Cream Cheese Frosting (page 11) (optional)

### chocolate sponge base

190 g plain flour
120 g caster sugar
40 g cocoa powder, plus extra to decorate
½ teaspoon bicarbonate of soda
40 ml sunflower oil
1½ teaspoons white vinegar
½ teaspoon vanilla extract

### cheesecake filling

140 g cream cheese
60 g caster sugar
1 egg
½ teaspoon vanilla extract
a pinch of salt
100 g milk chocolate chips

*a 12-hole cupcake tray, lined with paper cases (see note on page 4)*

Makes 12

Preheat the oven to 170°C (325°F) Gas 3.

**For the chocolate sponge base:** Put the flour, sugar, cocoa powder and bicarbonate of soda in a large bowl and mix with a handheld electric whisk on slow speed until all the dry ingredients are well incorporated.

Put the oil, vinegar, vanilla extract and 125 ml water in a jug and whisk to combine. While the electric whisk is running in the flour bowl, slowly add the contents of the jug, increasing the speed of the blender as the mixture thickens. Continue to beat until all the ingredients are incorporated (scrape any unmixed ingredients from the side of the bowl with a rubber spatula).

Spoon the mixture into the paper cases until two-thirds full and set aside.

**For the cheesecake filling:** Beat together the cream cheese, sugar, egg, vanilla extract and salt in a freestanding electric mixer with a paddle attachment (or use a handheld electric whisk) on medium-slow speed until smooth and fluffy.

Stir in the chocolate chips by hand until evenly dispersed. Don't overmix, otherwise the cream cheese will start to split.

Scoop about 1 tablespoon of the cheesecake filling on top of the cupcake mixture in the cases and bake in the preheated oven for about 20 minutes, or until the cupcakes are firm to the touch and they have an even golden colour on the cheesecake filling. Don't overcook as the cheesecake will become very dry and crumbly. Leave the cupcakes to cool slightly in the tray before turning out onto a wire cooling rack to cool completely.

When the cupcakes are cold, spoon the Cream Cheese Frosting on top, if using, and decorate with a light sprinkling of cocoa powder.

# lavender cupcakes

Many people can't imagine eating a lavender-infused cake, but this flavour is very popular in the summer. Infusing the milk with lavender flowers makes the flavour subtle. The icing can be left plain, or you can use a bit of food colouring to give it a light lavender colour.

120 ml whole milk
3 tablespoons dried lavender flowers
120 g plain flour
140 g caster sugar
1½ teaspoons baking powder
40 g unsalted butter, at room temperature
1 egg
12 small sprigs of lavender (optional)

**lavender frosting**
25 ml whole milk
1 tablespoon dried lavender flowers
250 g icing sugar, sifted
80 g unsalted butter, at room temperature
a couple of drops of purple food colouring (optional)

*a 12-hole cupcake tray, lined with paper cases (see note on page 4)*

Makes 12

Put the milk and dried lavender flowers in a jug, cover and refrigerate for a few hours, or overnight if possible. Do the same with the milk and lavender flowers for the frosting, in a separate jug.

Preheat the oven to 170°C (325°F) Gas 3.

Put the flour, sugar, baking powder and butter in a freestanding electric mixer with a paddle attachment (or use a handheld electric whisk) and beat on slow speed until you get a sandy consistency and everything is combined.

Strain the lavender-infused milk (for the cupcake) and slowly pour into the flour mixture, beating well until all the ingredients are well mixed. Add the egg and beat well (scrape any unmixed ingredients from the side of the bowl with a rubber spatula).

Spoon the mixture into the paper cases until two-thirds full and bake in the preheated oven for 20–25 minutes, or until the sponge bounces back when touched. A skewer inserted in the centre should come out clean. Leave the cupcakes to cool slightly in the tray before turning out onto a wire cooling rack to cool completely.

**For the lavender frosting:** Beat together the icing sugar, butter and food colouring, if using, in a freestanding electric mixer with a paddle attachment (or use a handheld electric whisk) on medium-slow speed until the mixture comes together and is well mixed. Turn the mixer down to slow speed. Strain the lavender-infused milk and slowly pour into the butter mixture. Once all the milk is incorporated, turn the mixer up to high speed. Continue beating until the frosting is light and fluffy, at least 5 minutes. The longer the frosting is beaten, the fluffier and lighter it becomes.

When the cupcakes are cold, spoon the lavender frosting on top and decorate with a sprig of lavender, if using.

# hazelnut and chocolate cupcakes

**Sometimes chocolate alone just won't do, which is why we've added irresistible hazelnut chocolate spread to these cupcakes. Decorate with hazelnuts for extra crunch.**

100 g plain flour

20 g cocoa powder

140 g caster sugar

1½ teaspoons baking powder

a pinch of salt

40 g butter, at room temperature

120 ml whole milk

1 egg

120 g hazelnut and chocolate spread (such as Nutella)

about 36 whole, shelled hazelnuts, to decorate

### hazelnut and chocolate frosting

250 g icing sugar, sifted

80 g unsalted butter, at room temperature

25 ml whole milk

80 g hazelnut and chocolate spread (such as Nutella)

*a 12-hole cupcake tray, lined with paper cases (see note on page 4)*

**Makes 12**

Preheat the oven to 170°C (325°F) Gas 3.

Put the flour, cocoa powder, sugar, baking powder, salt and butter in a freestanding electric mixer with a paddle attachment (or use a handheld electric whisk) and beat on slow speed until you get a sandy consistency and everything is combined.

Slowly pour the milk into the flour mixture, beating well until all the ingredients are well mixed. Add the egg and beat well (scrape any unmixed ingredients from the side of the bowl with a rubber spatula).

Spoon the mixture into the paper cases until two-thirds full and bake in the preheated oven for about 20 minutes, or until the sponge bounces back when touched. Leave the cupcakes to cool slightly in the tray before turning out onto a wire cooling rack to cool completely.

When the cupcakes are cold, hollow out a small section in the centre of each one and fill with a dollop of hazelnut and chocolate spread.

**For the hazelnut and chocolate frosting:** Beat the icing sugar and butter together in a freestanding electric mixer with a paddle attachment (or use a handheld electric whisk) on medium-slow speed until the mixture comes together and is well mixed. Turn the mixer down to a slower speed. Slowly pour in the milk, then when it is all incorporated, turn the mixer up to high speed. Continue beating until the frosting is light and fluffy, at least 5 minutes. The longer the frosting is beaten, the fluffier and lighter it becomes.

Stir in the hazelnut and chocolate spread by hand until evenly mixed into the frosting. When the cupcakes are cold, spoon the frosting on top and finish with about 3 hazelnuts per cupcake.

# coconut and pineapple cupcakes

Coconut and pineapple give these cupcakes a tropical flavour. Grated fresh coconut can be used instead of desiccated coconut for an even better flavour.

120 g plain flour

140 g caster sugar

1½ teaspoons baking powder

a pinch of salt

40 g unsalted butter, at room temperature

120 ml coconut milk

½ teaspoon vanilla extract

1 egg

9 tinned pineapple rings, chopped into small pieces

desiccated coconut, to decorate

**coconut frosting**

250 g icing sugar, sifted

80 g unsalted butter, at room temperature

25 ml coconut milk

*a 12-hole cupcake tray, lined with paper cases (see note on page 4)*

**Makes 12**

Preheat the oven to 170°C (325°F) Gas 3.

Put the flour, sugar, baking powder, salt and butter in a freestanding electric mixer with a paddle attachment (or use a handheld electric whisk) and beat on slow speed until you get a sandy consistency and everything is combined.

Mix the coconut milk and vanilla extract in a separate bowl, then beat into the flour mixture on medium speed until well combined. Add the egg and beat well (scrape any unmixed ingredients from the side of the bowl with a rubber spatula).

Divide the chopped pineapple between the paper cases. Spoon the cupcake mixture on top until two-thirds full and bake in the preheated oven for 20–25 minutes, or until light golden and the sponge bounces back when touched. A skewer inserted in the centre should come out clean. Leave the cupcakes to cool slightly in the tray before turning out onto a wire cooling rack to cool completely.

**For the coconut frosting:** Beat the icing sugar and butter together in a freestanding electric mixer with a paddle attachment (or use a handheld electric whisk) on medium-slow speed until the mixture comes together and is well mixed. Turn the mixer down to a slower speed and slowly pour in the coconut milk. Once all the milk has been incorporated, turn the mixer up to high speed. Continue beating until the frosting is very white, light and fluffy, 5–10 minutes.

When the cupcakes are cold, spoon the coconut frosting on top and finish with a sprinkling of desiccated coconut.

# banana and chocolate cupcakes

**Bananas work so well when used in baking, as they become almost caramel-like when they cook. Chocolate Frosting works particularly well with these, but Vanilla or Cream Cheese (see page 11) can also be used.**

120 g plain flour

140 g caster sugar

1 tablespoon baking powder

1 teaspoon ground cinnamon

1 teaspoon ground ginger

a pinch of salt

80 g unsalted butter, at room temperature

120 ml whole milk

2 eggs

120 g peeled banana, mashed

1 quantity Chocolate Frosting (page 11)

40 g dark chocolate, grated with a cheese grater into shavings

*a 12-hole cupcake tray, lined with paper cases (see note on page 4)*

**Makes 12**

Preheat the oven to 170°C (325°F) Gas 3.

Put the flour, sugar, baking powder, cinnamon, ginger, salt and butter in a freestanding electric mixer with a paddle attachment (or use a handheld electric whisk) and beat on slow speed until you get a sandy consistency and everything is combined.

Slowly pour the milk into the flour mixture, beating well until all the ingredients are well mixed. Add the eggs and beat well (scrape any unmixed ingredients from the side of the bowl with a rubber spatula).

Stir in the mashed banana by hand until evenly dispersed.

Spoon the mixture into the paper cases until two-thirds full and bake in the preheated oven for about 20 minutes, or until light golden and the sponge bounces back when touched. Leave the cupcakes to cool slightly in the tray before turning out onto a wire cooling rack to cool completely.

When the cupcakes are cold, spoon the Chocolate Frosting on top and finish with the chocolate shavings.

# green tea cupcakes

Green tea-flavoured desserts are very popular in Japan. Green tea works so well in cakes, combined with either vanilla or chocolate. It's important to use green tea powder called 'Matcha'. Buy it from tea shops and specialist Asian supermarkets.

120 ml whole milk

3 green tea bags

100 g plain flour

20 g cocoa powder

140 g caster sugar

1½ teaspoons baking powder

a pinch of salt

40 g unsalted butter, at room temperature

1 egg

¼ teaspoon vanilla extract

**green tea frosting**

250 g icing sugar, sifted

80 g unsalted butter, at room temperature

20 g Matcha green tea powder, plus extra to decorate

25 ml whole milk

*a 12-hole cupcake tray, lined with paper cases (see note on page 4)*

**Makes 12**

Put the milk and green tea bags in a jug, cover and refrigerate for a few hours, or overnight if possible.

Preheat the oven to 170°C (325°F) Gas 3.

Put the flour, cocoa powder, sugar, baking powder, salt and butter in a freestanding electric mixer with a paddle attachment (or use a handheld electric whisk) and beat on slow speed until you get a sandy consistency and everything is combined.

Remove the green tea bags from the infused milk and combine with the egg and vanilla extract. Slowly pour half into the flour mixture, beating well until all the ingredients are well mixed. Turn the mixer up to high speed and beat well to make sure there are no lumps. Turn the speed back down to medium-slow and slowly pour in the remaining milk mixture (scrape any unmixed ingredients from the side of the bowl with a rubber spatula). Continue mixing for a couple more minutes until the mixture is smooth.

Spoon the mixture into the paper cases until two-thirds full and bake in the preheated oven for 20–25 minutes, or until the sponge bounces back when touched. A skewer inserted in the centre should come out clean. Leave the cupcakes to cool slightly in the tray before turning out onto a wire cooling rack to cool completely.

**For the green tea frosting:** Beat together the icing sugar, butter and Matcha powder in a freestanding electric mixer with a paddle attachment (or use a handheld electric whisk) on medium-slow speed until the mixture comes together and is well mixed. Turn the mixer down to a slower speed. Slowly pour in the milk, then when it is all incorporated, turn the mixer up to high speed. Continue beating until the frosting is light and fluffy, at least 5 minutes.

When the cupcakes are cold, spoon the frosting on top and decorate with a light sprinkling of Matcha powder.

# peaches and cream cupcakes

**A classic summer combination – using fresh peaches makes the recipe work so much better. Other fruits in season could be substituted.**

120 g plain flour

140 g caster sugar

1½ teaspoons baking powder

a pinch of salt

40 g unsalted butter, at room temperature

120 ml whole milk

1 egg

¼ teaspoon vanilla extract

400 g tinned peaches, sliced

1 quantity Vanilla Frosting (page 11)

soft light brown sugar, to decorate (optional)

*a 12-hole cupcake tray, lined with paper cases (see note on page 4)*

**Makes 12**

Preheat the oven to 170°C (325°F) Gas 3.

Put the flour, sugar, baking powder, salt and butter in a freestanding electric mixer with a paddle attachment (or use a handheld electric whisk) and beat on slow speed until you get a sandy consistency and everything is combined. Gradually pour in half the milk and beat until the milk is just incorporated.

Whisk the egg, vanilla extract and remaining milk together in a separate bowl for a few seconds, then pour into the flour mixture and continue beating until just incorporated (scrape any unmixed ingredients from the side of the bowl with a rubber spatula). Continue mixing for a couple more minutes until the mixture is smooth. Do not overmix.

Divide the sliced peaches between the paper cases so that the base of each case is covered. Spoon the cupcake mixture on top until two-thirds full and bake in the preheated oven for 20–25 minutes, or until light golden and the sponge bounces back when touched. A skewer inserted in the centre should come out clean. Leave the cupcakes to cool slightly in the tray before turning out onto a wire cooling rack to cool completely.

When the cupcakes are cold, spoon the Vanilla Frosting on top and finish with a light sprinkling of soft light brown sugar, if using.

# pumpkin cupcakes

**These cupcakes are popular at Halloween and Thanksgiving. The light sprinkling of ground cinnamon over the Cream Cheese Frosting gives them a pretty finish.**

120 g plain flour

140 g caster sugar

1 tablespoon baking powder

1½ teaspoons ground cinnamon, plus extra to decorate

a pinch of salt

40 g unsalted butter, at room temperature

120 ml whole milk

2 eggs

200 g tinned pumpkin purée

1 quantity Cream Cheese Frosting (page 11)

*a 12-hole cupcake tray, lined with paper cases (see note on page 4)*

**Makes 12**

Preheat the oven to 170°C (325°F) Gas 3.

Put the flour, sugar, baking powder, cinnamon, salt and butter in a freestanding electric mixer with a paddle attachment (or use a handheld electric whisk) and beat on slow speed until you get a sandy consistency and everything is combined. Gradually pour in half the milk and beat until well mixed.

Add the eggs to the mix and beat well (scrape any unmixed ingredients from the side of the bowl with a rubber spatula). Stir in the pumpkin purée by hand until evenly dispersed.

Spoon the mixture into the paper cases until two-thirds full and bake in the preheated oven for about 20 minutes, or until light golden and the sponge bounces back when touched. Leave the cupcakes to cool slightly in the tray before turning out onto a wire cooling rack to cool completely.

When the cupcakes are cold, spoon the Cream Cheese Frosting on top and finish with a light sprinkling of cinnamon.

# marshmallow cupcakes

**Either Vanilla or Chocolate Frosting (see page 11) can be used to top these cupcakes, with bits of marshmallow to give texture. Crumbling digestive biscuits on top is a also good addition.**

120 g plain flour
140 g caster sugar
1½ teaspoons baking powder
a pinch of salt
45 g unsalted butter, at room temperature
120 ml whole milk
1 egg
¼ teaspoon vanilla extract
12 medium pink marshmallows
200 g mini marshmallows, for the frosting
1 quantity Vanilla Frosting (page 11)
edible glitter, to decorate

*a 12-hole cupcake tray, lined with paper cases (see note on page 4)*

**Makes 12**

Preheat the oven to 170°C (325°F) Gas 3.

Put the flour, sugar, baking powder, salt and butter in a freestanding electric mixer with a paddle attachment (or use a handheld electric whisk) and beat on slow speed until you get a sandy consistency and everything is combined. Gradually pour in half the milk and beat until the milk is just incorporated.

Whisk the egg, vanilla extract and remaining milk together in a separate bowl for a few seconds, then pour into the flour mixture and continue beating until just incorporated (scrape any unmixed ingredients from the side of the bowl with a rubber spatula). Continue mixing for a couple more minutes until the mixture is smooth. Do not overmix.

Spoon the mixture into the paper cases until two-thirds full and bake in the preheated oven for 20–25 minutes, or until light golden and the sponge bounces back when touched. A skewer inserted in the centre should come out clean. Leave the cupcakes to cool slightly in the tray before turning out onto a wire cooling rack to cool completely.

Put the medium marshmallows in a heatproof bowl over a pan of simmering water. Leave until melted and smooth. When the cupcakes are cold, hollow out a small section in the centre of each one and fill with a dollop of melted marshmallow. Leave to cool.

Stir the mini marshmallows into the Vanilla Frosting by hand until evenly dispersed.

Spoon the frosting on top of the cupcakes and decorate with edible glitter.

# ginger cupcakes

**These spicy cupcakes, moistened with ginger syrup, are perfect in winter.**

120 g plain flour

140 g caster sugar

1½ teaspoons baking powder

½ teaspoon ground cinnamon

¼ teaspoon ground allspice

a pinch of salt

40 g unsalted butter, at room temperature

120 ml whole milk

1 egg

¼ teaspoon vanilla extract

200 g stem ginger in syrup, finely chopped (and syrup reserved), plus extra to decorate

**ginger frosting**

100 ml whole milk

1 large piece of fresh ginger, peeled and chopped into 4 chunks

400 g icing sugar, sifted

125 g unsalted butter, at room temperature

grated zest of ½ unwaxed lemon, plus extra to decorate

*a 12-hole cupcake tray, lined with paper cases (see note on page 4)*

**Makes 12**

For the ginger frosting, put the milk and ginger pieces in a jug, cover and refrigerate for a few hours, or overnight if possible.

Preheat the oven to 170°C (325°F) Gas 3.

Put the flour, sugar, baking powder, cinnamon, allspice, salt and butter in a freestanding electric mixer with a paddle attachment (or use a handheld electric whisk) and beat on slow speed until you get a sandy consistency and everything is combined. Gradually pour in half the milk and beat until just incorporated. Whisk the egg, vanilla extract and remaining milk together in a separate bowl for a few seconds, then pour into the flour mixture and continue beating until just incorporated (scrape any unmixed ingredients from the side of the bowl with a rubber spatula). Continue mixing for a couple more minutes until the mixture is smooth. Stir in the chopped ginger by hand until evenly dispersed.

Spoon the mixture into the paper cases until two-thirds full and bake in the preheated oven for 20–25 minutes, or until golden brown and the sponge bounces back when touched. While the cupcakes are baking, pour 100 ml of the reserved ginger syrup and 100 ml water into a small saucepan and bring to the boil. Boil until reduced by one-third. When the hot cupcakes come out of the oven, pour a small amount of syrup over each one. Leave the cupcakes to cool slightly in the tray before turning out onto a wire cooling rack to cool completely.

**For the ginger frosting:** Beat together the icing sugar, butter and lemon zest in a freestanding electric mixer with a paddle attachment (or use a handheld electric whisk) on medium-slow speed until the mixture comes together and is well mixed. Turn the mixer down to slow speed. Strain the ginger-infused milk and slowly pour into the butter mixture. Once all the milk has been incorporated, turn the mixer up to high speed. Continue beating until the frosting is light and fluffy, at least 5 minutes.

When the cupcakes are cold, spoon the ginger frosting on top and finish with chopped stem ginger and lemon zest.

# cakes

# hummingbird cake

This cake is slightly similar to our carrot cake – moist and packed with flavour – but contains bananas and pineapple instead of carrots. The traditional recipe calls for pecan nuts, but walnuts could also be used.

300 g caster sugar

3 eggs

300 ml sunflower oil

270 g peeled bananas, mashed

1 teaspoon ground cinnamon, plus extra to decorate

300 g plain flour

1 teaspoon bicarbonate of soda

½ teaspoon salt

¼ teaspoon vanilla extract

100 g tinned pineapple, chopped into small pieces

100 g shelled pecan nuts (or walnuts), chopped, plus extra, chopped and whole, to decorate

2 quantities Cream Cheese Frosting (page 11)

*three 20-cm cake tins, base-lined with greaseproof paper*

**Makes 10-12 slices**

Preheat the oven to 170°C (325°F) Gas 3.

Put the sugar, eggs, oil, banana and cinnamon in a freestanding electric mixer with a paddle attachment (or use a handheld electric whisk) and beat until all the ingredients are well incorporated (don't worry if the mixture looks slightly split). Slowly add the flour, bicarbonate of soda, salt and vanilla extract and continue to beat until everything is well mixed.

Stir in the chopped pineapple and pecan nuts by hand until evenly dispersed.

Pour the mixture into the prepared cake tins and smooth over with a palette knife. Bake in the preheated oven for 20–25 minutes, or until golden brown and the sponge bounces back when touched. Leave the cakes to cool slightly in the tins before turning out onto a wire cooling rack to cool completely.

When the cakes are cold, put one on a cake stand and spread about one-quarter of the Cream Cheese Frosting over it with a palette knife. Place a second cake on top and spread another quarter of the frosting over it. Top with the last cake and spread the remaining frosting over the top and sides. Finish with pecan nuts and a light sprinkling of cinnamon.

# carrot cake

Another bestseller at the Hummingbird, this carrot cake is moist and full of flavour. You can vary how finely you chop the nuts for the sponge, and pecan nuts or walnuts can be substituted freely. For an extra-special touch, decorate the top with mini carrots – these can either be formed by hand using sugar paste or piped on using orange buttercream frosting.

300 g soft light brown sugar
3 eggs
300 ml sunflower oil
300 g plain flour
1 teaspoon bicarbonate of soda
1 teaspoon baking powder
1 teaspoon ground cinnamon, plus extra to decorate
½ teaspoon ground ginger
½ teaspoon salt
¼ teaspoon vanilla extract
300 g carrots, grated
100 g shelled walnuts, chopped, plus extra, chopped and whole, to decorate
2 quantities Cream Cheese Frosting (page 11)

*three 20-cm cake tins, base-lined with greaseproof paper*

**Makes 10–12 slices**

Preheat the oven to 170°C (325°F) Gas 3.

Put the sugar, eggs and oil in a freestanding electric mixer with a paddle attachment (or use a handheld electric whisk) and beat until all the ingredients are well incorporated (don't worry if the mixture looks slightly split). Slowly add the flour, bicarbonate of soda, baking powder, cinnamon, ginger, salt and vanilla extract and continue to beat until well mixed.

Stir in the grated carrots and walnuts by hand until they are all evenly dispersed.

Pour the mixture into the prepared cake tins and smooth over with a palette knife. Bake in the preheated oven for 20–25 minutes, or until golden brown and the sponge bounces back when touched. Leave the cakes to cool slightly in the tins before turning out onto a wire cooling rack to cool completely.

When the cakes are cold, put one on a cake stand and spread about one-quarter of the Cream Cheese Frosting over it with a palette knife. Place a second cake on top and spread another quarter of the frosting over it. Top with the last cake and spread the remaining frosting over the top and sides. Finish with walnuts and a light sprinkling of cinnamon.

# coconut meringue cake

This is the ultimate coconut cake. Use fresh coconut for the best results. No yolks are used in the sponge, making it airy and light. The boiled, soft meringue frosting is as light as the sponge, and sprinkling grated coconut all over the top and sides of the cake makes it look extra special.

1 fresh coconut

430 g caster sugar

120 g unsalted butter, at room temperature

500 g plain flour

1 tablespoon baking powder

250 ml whole milk

1 teaspoon vanilla extract

3 egg whites

**meringue frosting**

200 g egg whites (from 6–7 eggs)

320 g caster sugar

¼ teaspoon vanilla extract

*three 20-cm cake tins, base-lined with greaseproof paper*

**Makes 10–12 slices**

Preheat the oven to 170°C (325°F) Gas 3.

Pierce the eyes of the coconut and strain the milk into a jug. Add water to make 250 ml and pour into a saucepan. Add 60 g of the sugar and bring to the boil, stirring frequently, then set aside to cool. Meanwhile, heat the drained coconut in the preheated oven for about 15 minutes. Crack open the coconut and scoop out the fruit from the shell. Trim off the brown skin with a sharp knife. Grate the coconut and set aside.

Put the butter and remaining sugar in a freestanding electric mixer with a paddle attachment (or use a handheld electric whisk) and cream until light and fluffy. In a separate bowl, mix the flour and baking powder. In another bowl, mix the milk and vanilla extract. Beat the flour mixture into the creamed butter alternately with the milk mixture (scrape any unmixed ingredients from the side of the bowl with a rubber spatula). Beat until well mixed. In yet another bowl, whisk the egg whites with a handheld electric whisk until stiff peaks form. Using a metal spoon, fold the egg whites into the cake mixture until well mixed but do not overmix. Pour into the prepared cake tins and smooth over with a palette knife. Bake in the preheated oven for 25–30 minutes. Leave to cool slightly in the tins before turning out onto a wire cooling rack to cool.

**For the meringue frosting:** Put the egg whites, sugar and 75 ml water in a heatproof bowl over a saucepan of simmering water. Beat slowly with an electric handheld whisk until stiff peaks form, about 7 minutes. Remove from the heat and beat in the vanilla extract. The frosting should be thick and glossy.

When the cakes are cold, put one on a serving plate and drizzle with coconut syrup. Spread one-fifth of the frosting over it with a palette knife and top with grated coconut. Repeat for the next cake, then top with the third and spread the remaining frosting over the top and sides. Cover with grated coconut.

# brooklyn blackout cake

This is a must for chocolate lovers. The filling and frosting are made from an eggless chocolate custard. When you make the custard, if you spread it on a thin tray and cover it with clingfilm, it will cool down more quickly. The cake looks amazing when covered with crumbled chocolate sponge, with the almost black custard peeking through. You can refrigerate the cake to set slightly before serving.

100 g unsalted butter, at room temperature
260 g caster sugar
2 eggs
¼ teaspoon vanilla extract
45 g cocoa powder
¾ teaspoon baking powder
¾ teaspoon bicarbonate of soda
a pinch of salt
170 g plain flour
160 ml whole milk

**chocolate custard**
500 g caster sugar
1 tablespoon golden syrup
125 g cocoa powder
200 g cornflour
85 g unsalted butter, cubed
½ teaspoon vanilla extract

*three 20-cm cake tins, base-lined with greaseproof paper*

**Makes 10–12 slices**

Preheat the oven to 170°C (325°F) Gas 3.

Put the butter and sugar in a freestanding electric mixer with a paddle attachment (or use a handheld electric whisk) and cream until light and fluffy. Add the eggs one at a time, mixing well and scraping any unmixed ingredients from the side of the bowl with a rubber spatula after each addition. Turn the mixer down to slow speed and beat in the vanilla extract, cocoa powder, baking powder, bicarbonate of soda and salt until well mixed. Add half the flour, then all the milk, and finish with the remaining flour. Mix well until everything is well combined.

Pour the mixture into the prepared cake tins and smooth over with a palette knife. Bake in the preheated oven for 25–30 minutes. Leave the cakes to cool slightly in the tins before turning out onto a wire cooling rack to cool completely.

**For the chocolate custard:** Put the sugar, golden syrup, cocoa powder and 600 ml water into a large saucepan and bring to the boil over medium heat, whisking occasionally.

Mix the cornflour with 120 ml water, then whisk into the cocoa mixture in the saucepan. Bring back to the boil, whisking constantly. Cook until very thick, about 10 minutes. Remove from the heat and stir in the butter and vanilla extract. Pour the custard into a bowl, cover with clingfilm and chill until very firm.

When the cakes are cold, using a serrated knife, slice a thin layer off one of the cakes. Put this layer in a food processor and process to make fine crumbs. Put one cake on a cake stand and spread about one-quarter of the chocolate custard over it with a palette knife. Place a second cake on top and spread another quarter of the custard over it. Top with the last cake and spread the remaining custard over the top and sides. Cover with the cake crumbs and chill for about 2 hours.

# lemon and poppy seed cake

**A moist, tangy cake that is perfect with your afternoon cup of tea.**

125 g unsalted butter, at room temperature

370 g caster sugar

grated zest of 2 unwaxed lemons

25 g poppy seeds, plus extra to decorate

250 ml whole milk

560 g plain flour

1 tablespoon baking powder

1 teaspoon salt

4 egg whites

**lemon syrup**

freshly squeezed juice of 2 lemons

400 g caster sugar

**lemon glaze**

freshly squeezed juice of 1 lemon

250 g icing sugar, sifted

*a 25-cm ring mould, greased and dusted with flour*

**Makes 12–16 slices**

Preheat the oven to 170°C (325°F) Gas 3.

Put the butter, sugar, lemon zest and poppy seeds in a freestanding electric mixer with a paddle attachment (or use a handheld electric whisk) and beat until all the ingredients are well incorporated (don't worry if the mixture looks slightly split). Slowly add the milk and continue to beat until incorporated (don't worry if the mixture looks slightly split).

In a separate bowl, combine the flour, baking powder and salt. Add the flour mixture to the butter mixture in 3 additions, scraping any unmixed ingredients from the side of the bowl with a rubber spatula after each addition. Beat thoroughly until all the ingredients are well incorporated and the mixture is light and fluffy.

In a separate bowl, whisk the egg whites with a handheld electric whisk until stiff peaks form. Using a metal spoon, fold the whisked egg whites into the cake mixture until well mixed but do not overmix. Pour into the prepared ring mould and smooth over with a palette knife. Bake in the preheated oven for about 40 minutes, or until the sponge bounces back when touched.

**For the lemon syrup:** While the cake is baking, put the lemon juice, sugar and 500 ml water in a small saucepan and bring to the boil over low heat. Boil until it has reduced by half, or until it has a thin syrup consistency. When the hot cake comes out of the oven, pour the syrup all over the top. Leave to cool slightly in the mould before turning out onto a wire cooling rack to cool completely.

**For the lemon glaze:** Mix the lemon juice and icing sugar in a bowl until smooth. It should be thick but pourable – add a little water or more sugar to thin or thicken as necessary.

When the cake is cold, put it on a cake stand, pour the glaze over it and decorate with poppy seeds.

# blueberry cake

**Blueberries work so well in cakes, as they become soft and juicy and a wonderful deep purple. This cake is moist enough to be served without the frosting if you prefer.**

350 g unsalted butter, at room temperature

350 g caster sugar

6 eggs

1 teaspoon vanilla extract

450 g plain flour

2 tablespoons plus 2 teaspoons baking powder

280 ml soured cream

250 g fresh blueberries, plus extra to decorate

2 quantities Cream Cheese Frosting (page 11)

icing sugar, to decorate

*a 25-cm ring mould, greased and dusted with flour*

**Makes 12–16 slices**

Preheat the oven to 170°C (325°F) Gas 3.

Put the butter and sugar in a freestanding electric mixer with a paddle attachment (or use a handheld electric whisk) and cream until light and fluffy. Add the eggs one at a time, mixing well and scraping any unmixed ingredients from the side of the bowl with a rubber spatula after each addition. Beat in the vanilla extract, flour and baking powder until well mixed. Add the soured cream and mix well until everything is combined and the mixture is light and fluffy.

Gently stir in the blueberries by hand until evenly dispersed.

Pour the mixture into the prepared ring mould and smooth over with a palette knife. Bake in the preheated oven for 40 minutes, or until golden brown and the sponge bounces back when touched. Leave the cake to cool slightly in the mould before turning out onto a wire cooling rack to cool completely.

When the cake is cold, put it on a serving plate, cover the top and sides with the Cream Cheese Frosting and decorate with more blueberries. Dust with a light sprinkling of icing sugar.

# coffee cake

This is less sweet than some of the other cakes in this chapter, but you could top it with Chocolate Frosting (see page 11) to turn into a mocha cake for a sweeter tooth.

2 tablespoons instant coffee granules

450 g unsalted butter, at room temperature

450 g caster sugar

8 eggs

450 g plain flour

2 tablespoons baking powder

2 teaspoons cocoa powder, plus extra to decorate

1 quantity Vanilla Frosting (page 11)

60 g dark chocolate, grated with a cheese grater into shavings

coffee beans, to decorate (optional)

*a 25-cm ring mould, greased and dusted with flour*

**Makes 12–16 slices**

To make a coffee essence, put the instant coffee granules and 170 ml water in a small saucepan and bring to the boil over medium heat. Boil until reduced by half, then remove from the heat and leave to cool completely. Set aside a tablespoon of the essence to use in the frosting.

Preheat the oven to 170°C (325°F) Gas 3.

Put the butter, sugar and cold coffee essence in a freestanding electric mixer with a paddle attachment (or use a handheld electric whisk) and beat until all the ingredients are well incorporated. Add the eggs one at a time, mixing well and scraping any unmixed ingredients from the side of the bowl with a rubber spatula after each addition. Beat in the flour, baking powder and cocoa powder and mix well until everything is combined and the mixture is light and fluffy.

Pour the mixture into the prepared ring mould and smooth over with a palette knife. Bake in the preheated oven for 40 minutes, or until the sponge feels firm to the touch. (Do not open the oven while the cake is baking, as it will sink.) Leave the cake to cool slightly in the mould before turning out onto a wire cooling rack to cool completely.

Stir the reserved tablespoon of coffee essence into the Vanilla Frosting until evenly mixed.

When the cake is cold, put it on a serving plate, cover the top with the frosting and dust with a light sprinkling of cocoa powder. Decorate with the chocolate shavings and coffee beans, if using.

# spiced pound cake

**This is more flavourful than a regular pound cake, with lots of spices to liven it up. It's another not-too-sweet cake that's perfect with a cup of tea or coffee.**

230 g unsalted butter, at room temperature

650 g caster sugar

5 eggs

240 ml whole milk

1 teaspoon vanilla extract

¼ teaspoon lemon extract

¼ teaspoon ground cloves

¼ teaspoon ground cinnamon

¼ teaspoon ground ginger

¼ teaspoon ground nutmeg

400 g plain flour

½ teaspoon bicarbonate of soda

½ teaspoon salt

*a 25-cm ring mould, greased and dusted with flour*

**Makes 12–16 slices**

Preheat the oven to 170°C (325°F) Gas 3.

Put the butter and sugar in a freestanding electric mixer with a paddle attachment (or use a handheld electric whisk) and cream until light and fluffy. Add the eggs one at a time, mixing well and scraping any unmixed ingredients from the side of the bowl with a rubber spatula after each addition. Beat in the milk, vanilla extract and lemon extract until well mixed.

Sift the cloves, cinnamon, ginger, nutmeg, flour, bicarbonate of soda and salt into a separate bowl, then add to the butter mixture and beat until all the ingredients are well combined.

Pour the mixture into the prepared ring mould and smooth over with a palette knife. Bake in the preheated oven for 60–70 minutes, or until golden brown and a skewer inserted in the cake comes out clean. Leave to cool slightly in the mould before turning out onto a wire cooling rack to cool completely.

# buttermilk pound loaf

Here's a reliable, traditional pound cake recipe – moist with butter and not too sweet. You can add chocolate chips, nuts or berries to the cake mixture as an alternative.

120 g unsalted butter, at room temperature
330 g caster sugar
3 eggs
200 g plain flour
½ teaspoon bicarbonate of soda
½ teaspoon salt
120 ml buttermilk
¼ teaspoon vanilla extract

*a 23 x 13-cm loaf tin, greased and dusted with flour*

**Makes 8–10 slices**

Preheat the oven to 170°C (325°F) Gas 3.

Put the butter and sugar in a freestanding electric mixer with a paddle attachment (or use a handheld electric whisk) and cream until light and fluffy. Add the eggs one at a time, mixing well and scraping any unmixed ingredients from the side of the bowl with a rubber spatula after each addition.

Sift the flour, bicarbonate of soda and salt into a separate bowl. Add one-third of the flour mixture to the butter mixture, followed by half the buttermilk. Mix well. Repeat this process, then finish with the remaining flour mixture. Stir in the vanilla extract. Mix well until all the ingredients are well combined.

Pour the mixture into the prepared loaf tin and smooth over with a palette knife. Bake in the preheated oven for 35–40 minutes, or until golden brown and the sponge bounces back when touched. Leave the cake to cool slightly in the tin before turning out onto a wire cooling rack to cool completely.

# banana loaf

We get through several of these loaves every day in the Bakery. Try to use very ripe bananas for a sweeter, richer cake. You can also use light muscovado sugar, making the cake even more moist and rich.

270 g soft light brown sugar

2 eggs

200 g peeled bananas, mashed

280 g plain flour

1 teaspoon baking powder

1 teaspoon bicarbonate of soda

1 teaspoon ground cinnamon

1 teaspoon ground ginger

140 g unsalted butter, melted

*a 23 x 13-cm loaf tin, greased and dusted with flour*

**Makes 8–10 slices**

Preheat the oven to 170°C (325°F) Gas 3.

Put the sugar and eggs in a freestanding electric mixer with a paddle attachment (or use a handheld electric whisk) and beat until well incorporated. Beat in the mashed bananas.

Add the flour, baking powder, bicarbonate of soda, cinnamon and ginger to the sugar mixture. Mix it thoroughly until all the dry ingredients have been incorporated into the egg mixture. Pour in the melted butter and beat until all the ingredients are well mixed.

Pour the mixture into the prepared loaf tin and smooth over with a palette knife. Bake in the preheated oven for about 1 hour, or until firm to the touch and a skewer inserted in the centre comes out clean. Leave the cake to cool slightly in the tin before turning out onto a wire cooling rack to cool completely.

# nutty apple loaf

This cake is very popular in the winter months. We use chopped mixed nuts, but you could use your own combination of favourite nuts. The chunks of cooked apple in the cake give it a wonderful texture and flavour.

175 g unsalted butter, at room temperature

140 g soft light brown sugar

2 tablespoons strawberry jam

2 eggs

140 g plain flour

1 tablespoon baking powder

1 teaspoon ground cinnamon

100 g shelled mixed nuts, chopped

50 g dark chocolate, roughly chopped

2 eating apples, peeled, cored and roughly chopped

*a 23 x 13-cm loaf tin, greased and dusted with flour*

**Makes 8–10 slices**

Put the butter, sugar and strawberry jam in a freestanding electric mixer with a paddle attachment (or use a handheld electric whisk) and cream until light and fluffy. Add the eggs one at a time, mixing well and scraping any unmixed ingredients from the side of the bowl with a rubber spatula after each addition.

Sift together the flour, baking powder and cinnamon in a separate bowl, then beat into the butter mixture. Stir the nuts, chocolate and apples into the mixture by hand until evenly dispersed. Cover and refrigerate for a few hours, or overnight if possible.

Preheat the oven to 170°C (325°F) Gas 3.

Pour the mixture into the prepared loaf tin and smooth over with a palette knife. Bake in the preheated oven for 50–60 minutes, or until brown and the sponge feels firm to the touch. A skewer inserted in the centre should come out clean, but for a little melted chocolate. Leave the cake to cool slightly in the tin before turning out onto a wire cooling rack to cool completely.

# lemon loaf

When drizzled with the lemon syrup, this is incredibly moist, tangy and flies off our counter when served in the shop.

320 g caster sugar

3 eggs

grated zest of 2 unwaxed lemons

560 g plain flour

1½ teaspoons baking powder

1 teaspoon salt

250 ml whole milk

½ teaspoon vanilla extract

200 g unsalted butter, melted

**lemon syrup**

freshly squeezed juice and grated zest of 2 lemons

100 g caster sugar

*a 23 x 13-cm loaf tin, greased and dusted with flour*

**Makes 8–10 slices**

Preheat the oven to 170°C (325°F) Gas 3.

Put the sugar, eggs and lemon zest in a freestanding electric mixer with a paddle attachment (or use a handheld electric whisk) and beat until well mixed.

Sift the flour, baking powder and salt into a separate bowl. Combine the milk and vanilla extract in another bowl. Add one-third of the flour mixture to the sugar mixture and beat well, then beat in one-third of the milk mixture. Repeat this process twice more until everything has been added. Turn the mixer up to high speed and beat until the mixture is light and fluffy.

Turn the mixer down to low speed, pour in the melted butter and beat until well incorporated.

Pour the mixture into the prepared loaf tin and smooth over with a palette knife. Bake in the preheated oven for about 45–55 minutes, or until golden brown and the sponge bounces back when touched.

**For the lemon syrup:** While the cake is baking, put the lemon juice and zest, sugar and 200 ml water in a small saucepan and bring to the boil over low heat. Boil until it has reduced by half, or until it has a thin syrup consistency. When the hot cake comes out of the oven, pour the syrup all over the top. Leave to cool slightly in the tin before turning out onto a wire cooling rack to cool completely.

# new york cheesecake

A plain baked New York cheesecake is always extremely popular. It's important not to overbeat the ingredients – stop mixing as soon as each ingredient you add is just incorporated. You may think the cake isn't fully baked when you take it out of the oven, but it will set into a perfect cheesecake overnight! You can also fold in chopped cookies, brownies or berries just before baking to make a flavoured cheesecake.

900 g cream cheese
190 g caster sugar
1 teaspoon vanilla extract
4 eggs

**base**
140 g plain flour
¼ teaspoon baking powder
50 g caster sugar
50 g unsalted butter
1 egg yolk

*a 23-cm round springform cake tin, greased and base-lined with greaseproof paper*

**Makes 10–12 slices**

Preheat the oven to 150°C (300°F) Gas 2.

**For the base:** Put the flour, baking powder, sugar and butter in a freestanding electric mixer with a paddle attachment (or use a handheld electric whisk) and beat until you get a sandy consistency.

Add the egg yolk and mix through – it will still be sandy but it will be a little more moist. Press this mixture into the base of the prepared cake tin, using the ball of your hand or a tablespoon to flatten and compress it. It must be pressed down to form a dense base.

Bake in the preheated oven for 20–25 minutes, or until golden brown. It should have lost its sandy texture and come together to form a coherent base. Set aside to cool.

Put the cream cheese, sugar and vanilla extract in a freestanding electric mixer with a paddle attachment (or use a handheld electric whisk) and beat on slow speed until you get a very smooth, thick mixture. Add one egg at a time, while still mixing. Scrape any unmixed ingredients from the side of the bowl with a rubber spatula after adding the second and last eggs. The mixture should be very smooth and creamy. The mixer can be turned up to a higher speed at the end to make the mix a little lighter and fluffier, but be careful not to overmix otherwise the cheese will split.

Spoon the mixture onto the cold cheesecake base. Put the tin inside a larger tin or in a deep baking tray and fill with water until it reaches two-thirds of the way up the cake tin. Bake for 30–40 minutes, or until golden brown but still wobbly in the centre. Don't overcook. Leave the cheesecake to cool slightly in the tin, then cover and refrigerate overnight before serving.

# chocolate cheesecake

There must be a chocolate version of everything, so chocolate lovers don't have to miss out! Using the best-quality dark chocolate in this cheesecake will make the finished result taste so much better. A mix of triple chocolate chips (dark, milk and white) can be folded in before baking for an extra chocolate kick.

900 g cream cheese
190 g caster sugar
1 teaspoon vanilla extract
4 eggs
200 g dark chocolate, roughly chopped

**base**
200 g digestive biscuits
2 tablespoons cocoa powder
150 g unsalted butter, melted

*a 23-cm round springform cake tin, greased and base-lined with greaseproof paper*

**Makes 10–12 slices**

Preheat the oven to 150°C (300°F) Gas 2.

**For the base:** Roughly break up the digestive biscuits and put them in a food processor with the cocoa powder. Process until finely ground. Slowly pour the melted butter into the processor while the motor is running. Press this mixture into the base of the prepared cake tin, using the ball of your hand or a tablespoon to flatten and compress it. Refrigerate while you make the topping.

Put the cream cheese, sugar and vanilla extract in a freestanding electric mixer with a paddle attachment (or use a handheld electric whisk) and beat on slow speed until you get a very smooth, thick mixture. Add one egg at a time, while still mixing. Scrape any unmixed ingredients from the side of the bowl with a rubber spatula after adding the second and last eggs. The mixture should be very smooth and creamy. The mixer can be turned up to a higher speed at the end to make the mix a little lighter and fluffier, but be careful not to overmix otherwise the cheese will split.

Put the chocolate in a heatproof bowl over a saucepan of simmering water (do not let the base of the bowl touch the water). Leave until melted and smooth. Spoon a little of the cream cheese mixture into the melted chocolate, stir to mix, then add a little more. This will even out the temperatures of the 2 mixtures. Eventually stir all the cream cheese mixture into the chocolate mixture and mix until well combined and smooth.

Spoon the mixture onto the cold cheesecake base. Put the tin inside a larger tin or in a deep baking tray and fill with water until it reaches two-thirds of the way up the cake tin. Bake for 40–50 minutes, checking regularly after 40 minutes to make sure it isn't burning. Don't overcook – it should be wobbly in the centre. Leave the cheesecake to cool slightly in the tin, then cover and refrigerate overnight before serving.

# fridge-set banana cheesecake

This is another take on a cheesecake, but it is set and has a firmer texture than baked cheesecake. This recipe contains gelatine, so vegetarians will have to use a vegetarian alternative and follow the manufacturer's instructions.

6 leaves of gelatine

200 g peeled bananas, mashed, plus extra, sliced, to decorate

70 ml orange juice

300 g cream cheese

110 g caster sugar

3 egg yolks

250 ml double cream

**base**

200 g digestive biscuits

150 g unsalted butter, melted

*a 23-cm round springform cake tin, greased and base-lined with greaseproof paper*

**Makes 10–12 slices**

**For the base:** Roughly break up the digestive biscuits and put them in a food processor. Process until finely ground. Slowly pour the melted butter into the processor while the motor is running. Press this mixture into the base of the prepared cake tin, using the ball of your hand or a tablespoon to flatten and compress it. Refrigerate while you make the topping.

Put the gelatine leaves in a small jug of barely tepid water and soak according to the manufacturer's instructions.

Put the mashed bananas and orange juice in a saucepan and heat over medium heat until the bananas are cooked though. Set aside to cool slightly.

Put the cream cheese, sugar and egg yolks in a freestanding electric mixer with a paddle attachment (or use a handheld electric whisk) and beat on slow speed until you get a very smooth, thick mixture.

In a separate bowl, using a handheld electric whisk, whip the cream until thick but not stiff. Gently fold into the cream cheese mixture by hand. Set aside.

Take the soaked gelatine leaves out of the jug and put into the warm banana and orange juice mixture – make sure the banana mixture is just warm and not hot, as high heat can destroy the gelatine. Stir well until all the gelatine has completely melted and is evenly dispersed. Spoon a little of the cream cheese mixture into the banana mixture and stir to mix, then add a little more. This will even out the temperatures of the 2 mixtures and prevent the gelatine from setting in lumps. Eventually stir all the banana mixture into the cream cheese mixture and mix until well combined and smooth.

Spoon the mixture onto the cold cheesecake base and leave to cool completely. Cover and refrigerate for 2 hours, or overnight if possible. Decorate with slices of banana before serving.

# pies

# basic pie crust

This simple pie crust is used in most of the recipes in this chapter. You will either need to bake it blind and top with a pie filling that doesn't need any further baking, or if the filling needs to be cooked, then only partially blind bake the crust.

260 g plain flour
½ teaspoon salt
110 g unsalted butter

*a 23-cm pie dish, greased*
*baking beans*

**Makes enough for a 23-cm pie dish**

Put the flour, salt and butter in an electric mixer with a paddle attachment and beat on slow speed until you get a sandy consistency and everything is combined. Add 1 tablespoon water and beat until well mixed. Add a second tablespoon of water and beat until you have a smooth, even dough. If the dough is still a little dry, add another tablespoon of water, but be careful not to add too much water – it is safer to beat the dough at high speed to try to bring the ingredients together.

Wrap the dough in clingfilm and leave to rest for 1 hour.

Preheat the oven to 170°C (325°F) Gas 3.

Lightly dust a clean work surface with flour and roll out the dough with a rolling pin. Line the prepared pie dish with the dough and trim the edges with a sharp knife. Lay a sheet of greaseproof paper over the dough crust and pour in the baking beans.

**To blind bake (for a pie that WILL NOT need baking again):** Bake the pie crust in the preheated oven for about 15–20 minutes, or until the edges are light golden and partially cooked. Remove the greaseproof paper and baking beans and bake for a further 15–20 minutes. Take care not to overcook – the edges should be light golden.

**To partially blind bake (for a pie that WILL need baking again):** Bake the pie crust in the preheated oven for about 10 minutes. Remove the greaseproof paper and baking beans and bake for a further 10 minutes. The dough should still be pale and slightly raw in the centre.

# lemon meringue pie

This old favourite never lasts long when we put it out on our shelves! The meringue topping should be generous and tall. There are two options for making the meringue in the recipe below: the Italian is our authentic version, but the nervous baker can use the simpler version. Use a warm knife when cutting the pie – it keeps the slices neat. The sliced pie looks amazing with the bright yellow filling and white, fluffy topping.

8 egg yolks

2 x 397-g tins condensed milk

freshly squeezed juice and grated zest of 8 unwaxed lemons

1 Basic Pie Crust, partially blind baked (page 80)

**simpler meringue topping**

6 egg whites

330 g caster sugar

1 teaspoon vanilla extract

**OR Italian meringue topping**

400 g caster sugar

7 egg whites

¼ teaspoon vanilla extract

**Makes 10–12 slices**

Preheat the oven to 150°C (300°F) Gas 2.

Put the egg yolks, condensed milk and lemon juice and zest in a glass bowl and mix gently with a balloon whisk until all the ingredients are very well incorporated. The mixture will thicken naturally.

Pour into the partially blind-baked pie crust and bake in the preheated oven for 20–30 minutes. The filling should be firm to the touch but still very slightly soft in the centre (not wobbly!). Leave to cool completely, then cover and refrigerate for at least 1 hour, or overnight if possible.

**For the simpler meringue topping:** Preheat the oven to 150°C (300°F) Gas 2.

Put the egg whites in a freestanding electric mixer with a whisk attachment and whisk until frothy. Gradually add 2 tablespoons of the sugar at a time, whisking well after each addition. Once you have whisked in all the sugar, add the vanilla extract and whisk again until stiff peaks form.

Spoon the meringue on top of the cold pie, making sure you completely cover the pie filling. Create peaks and swirls in the top of the meringue with the back of a tablespoon.

Bake in the preheated oven for about 20 minutes, or until the meringue is golden brown and crisp to the touch. (With this method, the egg whites are not cooked through, so please see the note on page 4 about uncooked or partially cooked eggs.) Leave to cool completely before serving.

**For the Italian meringue topping:** Preheat the oven to 150°C (300°F) Gas 2.

Put the sugar in a small saucepan and just cover with water. Set over medium heat and bring to the boil.

While the sugar is on the hob, put the egg whites in a freestanding electric mixer with a whisk attachment (or use a handheld electric whisk) on medium-slow speed. Whisk until the egg whites are light and foamy. When the sugar has been boiling for a short while, it should reach soft ball stage (see below).

Turn the mixer up to medium-high speed and slowly pour the sugar syrup into the egg whites. Once all the syrup is incorporated, turn the mixer up to maximum speed and whisk for about 10–15 minutes, or until the meringue has tripled in size and is very white and fluffy. Turn the mixer back down to medium speed and continue to whisk for a couple more minutes until the meringue has cooled down slightly.

Spoon the meringue on top of the cold pie, making sure you completely cover the pie filling. Create peaks and swirls in the top of the meringue with the back of a tablespoon.

Bake in the preheated oven for about 20 minutes, or until the meringue is golden brown and crisp to the touch. Leave to cool completely before serving.

**Soft ball stage:** When the sugar has been boiling for a short while, the appearance of the bubbles starts to change from very watery to more syrupy. Dip a spoon into the sugar, then drop it directly into a glass of cold water. The sugar will firm up on contact with the water. You should be able to form a soft ball out of the sugar, in which case it has reached soft ball stage. If it sets too hard to be able to form a ball, it has been boiled too long and has reached hard ball stage. Be careful, as the sugar goes from soft ball stage to hard ball stage very quickly. Don't touch the hot syrup with your bare hands until you have dipped the spoon into the glass of cold water, otherwise you will burn your fingers!

# pecan pie

Here's another American must. For an authentic flavour, try to find corn syrup rather than resorting to golden syrup. The dark corn syrup used here can be found in some specialist food shops or through online suppliers of American ingredients.

1 quantity Basic Pie Crust dough, unbaked (page 80)

200 g caster sugar

250 ml dark corn syrup

½ teaspoon salt

3 eggs

60 g unsalted butter, cubed

¼ teaspoon vanilla extract

100 g shelled pecan nuts, chopped, plus extra pecan halves to decorate

*a 23-cm pie dish, greased*

**Makes 10–12 slices**

Preheat the oven to 170°C (325°F) Gas 3.

Lightly dust a clean work surface with flour and roll out the dough with a rolling pin. Line the prepared pie dish with the dough and trim the edges with a sharp knife.

Put the sugar, corn syrup and salt in a large saucepan over medium heat. Bring to the boil, then remove from the heat and leave to cool down slightly.

In a separate bowl, whisk the eggs briefly with a balloon whisk until they are just mixed. Slowly pour the warm (not hot) syrup into the eggs, stirring briskly so that you don't allow the eggs time to scramble.

Add the butter and vanilla extract to the bowl and stir until the butter has melted and is evenly dispersed.

Put the chopped pecan nuts into the pie crust, then pour the filling on top. Arrange the pecan halves gently on top of the filling around the edge of the pie. Bake in the preheated oven for about 50–60 minutes, or until a dark, caramel colour with a slightly crusty surface.

# key lime pie

We don't use any food colouring in our lime filling, just a bit of lime zest. Our Key Lime Pie is topped with a mound of freshly whipped cream, but you can use the same meringue as the Lemon Meringue Pie (see pages 81–82).

8 egg yolks

2 x 397-g tins condensed milk

freshly squeezed juice and grated zest of 5 limes, plus extra grated zest to decorate

450 ml whipping cream

### crust

500 g digestive biscuits

200 g unsalted butter, melted

*a 23-cm pie dish, greased*

**Makes 10–12 slices**

Preheat the oven to 170°C (325°F) Gas 3.

**For the crust:** Roughly break up the digestive biscuits and put them in a food processor. Process until finely ground. Slowly pour the melted butter into the processor while the motor is running. Press this mixture into the base and neatly up the side of the prepared pie dish, using the ball of your hand or a tablespoon to flatten and compress it.

Bake in the preheated oven for about 20 minutes, or until deep golden and firm. Set aside to cool completely.

Turn the oven down to 150°C (300°F) Gas 2.

Put the egg yolks, condensed milk and lime juice and zest in a glass bowl and mix gently with a balloon whisk until all the ingredients are very well incorporated. The mixture will thicken naturally.

Pour into the cold pie crust and bake in the preheated oven for 20–30 minutes. The filling should be firm to the touch but still very slightly soft in the centre (not wobbly!). Leave to cool completely, then cover and refrigerate for at least 1 hour, or overnight if possible.

When you are ready to serve the pie, whip the cream with a handheld electric whisk in a large bowl until soft peaks form, then spread over the pie and decorate with a little lime zest.

# pumpkin pie

The classic Thanksgiving pie, Pumpkin Pie is incredibly easy to make. The finished pie looks rustic and simple, with a deep golden-orange filling. If you don't want to leave it plain, you can cover it in whipped cream, but plain is more traditional.

1 quantity Basic Pie Crust dough, unbaked (page 80)

1 egg

425-g tin pumpkin purée

235 ml evaporated milk

220 g caster sugar

¼ teaspoon ground cloves

1 teaspoon salt

¾ teaspoon ground cinnamon, plus extra to decorate

¼ teaspoon ground ginger

1 tablespoon plain flour

lightly whipped cream, to serve (optional)

*a 23-cm pie dish, greased*

**Makes 10–12 slices**

Preheat the oven to 170°C (325°F) Gas 3.

Lightly dust a clean work surface with flour and roll out the dough with a rolling pin. Line the prepared pie dish with the dough and trim the edges with a sharp knife.

Put the egg, pumpkin purée, evaporated milk, sugar, cloves, salt, cinnamon, ginger and flour in a large bowl and mix with a wooden spoon until everything is well combined and there are no lumps.

Pour into the pie crust and bake in the preheated oven for about 30–40 minutes, or until the filling is set firm and doesn't wobble when shaken.

Leave to cool completely, then serve with a dollop of lightly whipped cream, if using, and a light sprinkling of cinnamon.

# mississippi mud pie

**Our version of Mississippi Mud Pie has a rich, cooked chocolate pudding filling, topped with a mountain of whipped cream. You can finish the pie with grated chocolate or cocoa powder. This is another pie that is extremely popular and sells out fast.**

150 g dark chocolate, roughly chopped, plus extra, grated with a cheese grater into shavings, to decorate

50 g unsalted butter

30 ml golden syrup

6 eggs

300 g soft light brown sugar

1 teaspoon vanilla extract

1 Basic Pie Crust, partially blind baked (page 80)

350 ml whipping cream

**Makes 10–12 slices**

Preheat the oven to 170°C (325°F) Gas 3.

Put the chocolate, butter and golden syrup in a heatproof bowl over a saucepan of simmering water (do not let the base of the bowl touch the water). Leave until melted and smooth, then remove from the heat and leave to cool slightly.

While the chocolate mixture is melting, put the eggs, sugar and vanilla extract in a freestanding electric mixer with a paddle attachment (or use a handheld electric whisk) and beat until well combined.

Gradually beat the warm chocolate mixture into the egg mixture on slow speed. Make sure the chocolate isn't too hot, otherwise it will scramble the eggs. Beat thoroughly until smooth.

Pour into the partially blind-baked pie crust and bake in the preheated oven for about 35–40 minutes. Check regularly after 30 minutes to make sure it isn't burning. The baked pie should be firm to the touch but still have a slight wobble in the centre. Leave to cool completely, then cover and refrigerate overnight.

When you are ready to serve the pie, whip the cream with a handheld electric whisk in a large bowl until soft peaks form, then spread over the pie and finish with chocolate shavings.

# banana cream pie

For this pie, you blind bake the pastry but the filling itself is not baked – the pie is simply filled with a custard full of banana chunks. As with all banana recipes, it's best to use very ripe bananas. Be generous with the whipped cream topping, and dust liberally with cinnamon. The base is covered with dulce de leche – a delicious South American soft caramel which is now easily found in supermarkets.

100 g dulce de leche

1 Basic Pie Crust, fully blind baked (page 80)

3 large bananas, peeled and sliced, plus extra to decorate

400 ml whipping cream

ground cinnamon, to decorate

**custard**

500 ml whole milk

¼ teaspoon vanilla extract

5 egg yolks

200 g caster sugar

40 g plain flour

40 g cornflour

**Makes 10–12 slices**

Preheat the oven to 170°C (325°F) Gas 3.

**For the custard:** Put 400 ml of the milk and the vanilla extract in a medium saucepan over medium heat and bring to the boil. Remove from the heat and leave to cool down very slightly.

Put the egg yolks, sugar, flour, cornflour and remaining milk in a separate bowl and mix well to form a smooth paste.

Pour a little of the hot milk mixture into the egg mixture and stir well to combine. Pour the remaining milk mixture into the egg mixture and stir well until all the ingredients are combined.

Pour everything back into the saucepan over low heat and bring to the boil, whisking continuously with a balloon whisk. Cook until thick, about 5 minutes. Pour the custard into a bowl, lay clingfilm directly on top (to stop a skin forming) and leave to cool completely.

Spread the dulce de leche over the base of the pie crust and arrange the slices of banana over it. Spoon the cold custard over the top. Cover and refrigerate for a couple of hours until the custard has set completely.

When you are ready to serve the pie, whip the cream with a handheld electric whisk in a large bowl until soft peaks form, then spread over the pie and decorate with more slices of banana. Finish with a generous sprinkling of cinnamon.

# apple pie

You can't go wrong with a slice of warm, classic apple pie served with a scoop of vanilla ice cream! For more skilled home-bakers, it's fun to decorate the top layer of pastry with cut-out leaves and other shapes. Be sure to brush the top with an egg wash and sprinkle with sugar to get a beautiful golden finish. Do also use firm, tart apples such as Granny Smiths, as they hold their shape and prevent the filling from becoming too sweet.

2 quantities Basic Pie Crust dough, unbaked (page 80)

150 g unsalted butter

3 teaspoons ground cinnamon

1.5 kg green apples, peeled, cored and cut into medium slices

200 g caster sugar, plus extra to sprinkle

1 egg, mixed with a little milk

*a 23-cm pie dish, greased*

**Makes 10–12 slices**

Preheat the oven to 170°C (325°F) Gas 3.

Lightly dust a clean work surface with flour. Divide the dough in half. Roll out one half with a rolling pin, use to line the prepared pie dish and trim the edges with a sharp knife.

Put the butter and cinnamon in a large saucepan and heat until the butter has melted. Add the apples and stir until they are well coated in butter. Finally, add the sugar and stir again. Cook the apples until softened but not cooked through, then spread them out on a tray to cool completely.

Fill the pie crust with the cold apples. Lightly dust a clean work surface with flour again. Roll out the remaining half of the dough with a rolling pin, drape over the pie dish and press down the edges, pinching to make a textured edge. Trim any excess with a sharp knife.

Make 3 slits in the lid of the pie to let the steam out while the pie is cooking. Make leaf shapes out of the pastry trimmings and use to decorate the pie. Brush the egg-and-milk wash over the top of the pie with a pastry brush and sprinkle with a little extra sugar. Bake in the preheated oven for about 30–40 minutes, or until the pastry is golden brown. Leave to cool completely before serving.

# blueberry pie

This is a summer favourite that should be made with lots of fresh, ripe blueberries. The cornflour thickens the filling as it cooks and keeps it firm enough to allow the pie to be sliced. The filling should bubble through the cuts made in the pastry lid, which is when you know the pie is ready.

2 quantities Basic Pie Crust dough, unbaked (page 80)

100 g caster sugar

25 g cornflour

2 tablespoons freshly squeezed lemon juice

2 teaspoons grated lemon zest

600 g blueberries

*a 23-cm pie dish, greased*

**Makes 10–12 slices**

Lightly dust a clean work surface with flour. Divide the dough in half. Roll out one half with a rolling pin, use to line the prepared pie dish and trim the edges with a sharp knife.

Put the sugar, cornflour, lemon juice and zest and blueberries in a bowl and mix well. Fill the pie crust with the blueberry mixture. Lightly dust a clean work surface with flour again. Roll out the remaining half of the dough with a rolling pin, drape over the pie dish and press down the edges, pinching to make a textured edge. Trim any excess with a sharp knife.

Make 3 slits in the lid of the pie to let the steam out while the pie is cooking. Leave the pie to rest in the refrigerator for 1 hour before baking.

Preheat the oven to 170°C (325°F) Gas 3.

Bake the pie in the preheated oven for about 40–50 minutes, or until the filling is bubbling thickly. After 30 minutes of baking, protect the edges from overcooking by covering them with foil. Leave to cool completely before serving.

# brownies and bars

## traditional brownie

Traditional brownies must be chewy, chocolatey and dense. Many other brownie recipes seen outside the USA are not really brownies! We don't put nuts in this traditional recipe, but you can add walnuts or pecan nuts if you like. These brownies are so popular in London, we sell several trays every day. For chocolate overload, you can put chocolate chips into the mixture before baking!

200 g dark chocolate, roughly chopped
175 g unsalted butter
325 g caster sugar
130 g plain flour
3 eggs
icing sugar, to decorate

*a 33 x 23 x 5-cm baking tray, lined with greaseproof paper*

**Makes about 12 portions**

Preheat the oven to 170°C (325°F) Gas 3.

Put the chocolate and butter in a heatproof bowl over a saucepan of simmering water (do not let the base of the bowl touch the water). Leave until melted and smooth.

Remove from the heat. Add the sugar and stir until well incorporated. Add the flour and stir until well incorporated. Finally, stir in the eggs and mix until thick and smooth.

Spoon the mixture into the prepared baking tray and bake in the preheated oven for about 30–35 minutes, or until flaky on the top but still soft in the centre. Be careful not to overcook otherwise the edges will become hard and crunchy. Leave to cool completely before dusting with icing sugar, to decorate.

# frosted brownie

Our alternative to the traditional brownie, this version is more cake-like, contains nuts and is topped with chocolatey cream-cheese frosting.

5 eggs
500 g caster sugar
120 g plain flour
100 g cocoa powder
250 g unsalted butter, melted
30 g shelled walnuts, chopped
30 g dark chocolate, roughly chopped

**frosting**
200 g icing sugar, sifted
75 g unsalted butter, at room temperature
30 g cocoa powder, sifted
150 g cream cheese, cold

*a 33 x 23 x 5-cm baking tray, lined with greaseproof paper*

**Makes about 12 portions**

Preheat the oven to 170°C (325°F) Gas 3.

Put the eggs and sugar in a large bowl and beat with a handheld electric whisk until light and fluffy. Add the flour and cocoa powder and beat until all the ingredients are well mixed. Pour in the melted butter and mix through. Stir the walnuts and chocolate in by hand until evenly dispersed.

Spoon the mixture into the prepared baking tray and bake in the preheated oven for about 30–35 minutes, or until the top is firm but the centre is still soft. Leave to cool completely.

**For the frosting:** Beat together the icing sugar, butter and cocoa powder in a freestanding electric mixer with a paddle attachment (or use a handheld electric whisk) on medium-slow speed until the mixture comes together and is well mixed. Add the cream cheese in one go and beat until it is completely incorporated. Turn the mixer up to medium-high speed. Continue beating until the frosting is light and fluffy, at least 5 minutes. Do not overbeat, as it can quickly become runny.

When the brownie is cold, spread the frosting over the top.

# raspberry cheesecake brownie

This triple-layer dessert looks irresistible when sliced: a slim layer of brownie topped with cheesecake and covered with raspberry-flavoured whipped cream. The three elements combine beautifully. You can substitute other berries in season if you like.

### brownie
200 g dark chocolate, roughly chopped
200 g unsalted butter
250 g icing sugar
3 eggs
110 g plain flour

### cheesecake
400 g cream cheese
150 g icing sugar
½ teaspoon vanilla extract
2 eggs

### cream topping
300 ml whipping cream
100 g icing sugar
150 g raspberries, plus extra to decorate

*a 33 x 23 x 5-cm baking tray, lined with greaseproof paper*

**Makes about 12 portions**

Preheat the oven to 170°C (325°F) Gas 3.

**For the brownie:** Put the chocolate in a heatproof bowl over a pan of simmering water (do not let the base of the bowl touch the water). Leave until melted and smooth. Put the butter and sugar in a freestanding electric mixer with a paddle attachment and beat until all the ingredients are well incorporated. Add the eggs one at a time, mixing well and scraping any unmixed ingredients from the side of the bowl with a rubber spatula after each addition. Gradually beat in the flour, mixing well after each addition, then turn the mixer up to high speed and beat for a little longer until you get a smooth mixture. Slowly pour in the melted chocolate and mix thoroughly. Pour into the prepared baking tray and smooth over with a palette knife.

**For the cheesecake:** Put the cream cheese, sugar and vanilla extract in a freestanding electric mixer with a paddle attachment and beat on slow speed until smooth and thick. Add one egg at a time, while still mixing. Scrape any unmixed ingredients from the side of the bowl with a rubber spatula after each addition. The mixture should be very smooth and creamy. The mixer can be turned up to a higher speed at the end to make the mix a little lighter and fluffier, but be careful not to overmix, otherwise the cheese will split. Spoon on top of the brownie and smooth over with a palette knife. Bake in the preheated oven for 30–40 minutes, or until the cheesecake is firm to the touch and light golden around the edges. The centre should still be pale. Leave to cool completely, then cover and refrigerate for 2 hours, or overnight if possible.

**For the cream topping:** Put the cream, sugar and raspberries in a freestanding electric mixer with a whisk attachment and beat until firm but not stiff. Turn the brownie out onto a board and turn the right way up. Spread the topping evenly over the brownie and decorate with more raspberries.

# blondie

**Here's an alternative to brownies for those who don't like the rich taste of chocolate; these blondies are made with white chocolate.**

150 g white chocolate, roughly chopped

125 g unsalted butter

150 g caster sugar

2 eggs

1½ teaspoons vanilla extract

200 g plain flour

a pinch of salt

120 g shelled pecan nuts, chopped

*a 33 x 23 x 5-cm baking tray, lined with greaseproof paper*

**Makes about 12 portions**

Preheat the oven to 170°C (325°F) Gas 3.

Put the chocolate and butter in a heatproof bowl over a saucepan of simmering water (do not let the base of the bowl touch the water). Leave until melted and smooth.

Remove from the heat. Add the sugar and stir until well incorporated. Add the eggs and vanilla extract, stirring briskly so that you don't allow the eggs time to scramble. Don't worry if the mixture looks like it is starting to split. Add the flour, salt and pecan nuts and stir until well incorporated and the nuts are evenly dispersed.

Spoon the mixture into the prepared baking tray and bake in the preheated oven for about 35–40 minutes, or until golden brown and the centre is still soft. Leave to cool completely.

# chocolate fridge cake bars

**A crunchy treat that requires no baking.**

400 g unsalted butter
200 ml golden syrup
100 g cocoa powder
800 g digestive biscuits, broken into small chunks
200 g raisins

*a 33 x 23 x 5-cm baking tray, lined with greaseproof paper*

**Makes about 12 portions**

Put the butter, golden syrup and cocoa powder in a large saucepan over medium heat and heat until melted and smooth, stirring occasionally.

Put the biscuit chunks and raisins in a large bowl and pour in the chocolate mixture. Mix with a wooden spoon until everything is well mixed and the biscuits and raisins are evenly dispersed.

Press this mixture into the prepared baking tray, using a tablespoon to flatten and compress it. Cover with a sheet of greaseproof paper, then a tray covered in jam jars or tins to apply pressure on the cake and compress it even more. Leave to cool completely, then refrigerate for a couple of hours, or overnight if possible.

# muesli bars

**These are packed with nuts, dried fruits and cereal. You can be flexible with the ingredients, and add your favourite nuts or dried fruits.**

320 g unsalted butter
240 ml golden syrup
250 g soft light brown sugar
250 g rolled oats
200 g desiccated coconut
125 g dried apricots, finely chopped
60 g dried dates, finely chopped
125 g cornflakes
125 g sunflower seeds
60 g dried cranberries
125 g shelled walnuts, chopped
125 g raisins

*a 33 x 23 x 5-cm baking tray, lined with greaseproof paper*

**Makes about 12 portions**

Put the butter, golden syrup and sugar in a large saucepan over medium heat and heat until melted and smooth, stirring occasionally.

Put the oats, coconut, apricots, dates, cornflakes, sunflower seeds, cranberries, walnuts and raisins in a large bowl and stir with a wooden spoon until everything is evenly mixed. Pour in the butter mixture and mix thoroughly until everything is well mixed and the dry ingredients are evenly dispersed.

Press this mixture into the prepared baking tray, using a tablespoon to flatten and compress it. Cover with a sheet of greaseproof paper, then a tray covered in jam jars or tins to apply pressure on the cake and compress it even more. Leave to cool, then refrigerate overnight.

**See photograph on page 110.**

# lemon bars

These bars are tangy and gooey. Dust with icing sugar, and make sure the bars are chilled so that they set before slicing.

210 g caster sugar
3 eggs
100 ml freshly squeezed lemon juice
3 teaspoons grated lemon zest

**base**
290 g plain flour
70 g icing sugar
a pinch of salt
230 g unsalted butter
2 teaspoons grated lemon zest

*a 33 x 23 x 5-cm baking tray, lined with greaseproof paper*

**Makes about 12 portions**

Preheat the oven to 170°C (325°F) Gas 3.

**For the base:** Put the flour, sugar, salt, butter and lemon zest in a freestanding electric mixer with a paddle attachment (or use a handheld electric whisk) and beat until the mixture resembles breadcrumbs. Press the dough together with your hands, then press it evenly into the base of the prepared baking tray. Bake in the preheated oven for about 20 minutes, or until light golden. (Leave the oven on.) Leave to cool slightly.

Put the sugar, eggs and lemon juice and zest in a bowl and whisk with a balloon whisk until well mixed. Pour carefully over the baked base and return to the oven. Bake for 20 minutes, or until the edges are golden brown and the topping has set. Leave to cool completely, then cover and refrigerate overnight.

**See photograph on page 111.**

# rocky road bars

Like the Chocolate Fridge Cake Bars on page 109, these Rocky Roads don't require baking. You can use any of your favourite chocolate bars. For cute, individual servings, scoop the mixture into muffin cases before refrigerating.

1.4 kg milk chocolate, roughly chopped
8 regular-sized chewy, filled chocolate bars of your choice (such as Snickers and Mars), roughly chopped
100 g marshmallows
180 g chocolate-coated malt honeycomb balls (such as Maltesers)
100 g dried apricots, roughly chopped
100 g raisins
100 g cornflakes
100 g chocolate vermicelli

*a 33 x 23 x 5-cm baking tray, lined with greaseproof paper*

**Makes about 12 generous portions**

Put the milk chocolate in a large saucepan over medium heat and heat until melted and smooth, stirring occasionally.

Put the chocolate bars, marshmallows, honeycomb balls, apricots, raisins and cornflakes in a large bowl and pour in the melted chocolate. Mix with a wooden spoon until everything is well mixed and the dry ingredients are evenly dispersed.

Press this mixture into the prepared baking tray, using a tablespoon to flatten and compress it. Sprinkle the chocolate vermicelli all over the top. Leave to cool completely, then cover and refrigerate overnight.

# muffins

## ham and mushroom muffins

**These savoury muffins are a good breakfast treat.**

50 g butter
½ small onion, finely chopped
80 g button mushrooms, chopped
360 g plain flour
2½ teaspoons baking powder
250 g Cheddar cheese, grated
220 ml whole milk
1 egg
80 g smoked ham, finely chopped
sea salt and freshly ground black pepper

*a 12-hole muffin tray, lined with paper cases*

**Makes 12**

Preheat the oven to 170°C (325°F) Gas 3.

Melt the butter in a saucepan over medium heat, then fry the onion and mushrooms until cooked. Season with sea salt and black pepper. Set aside.

Put the flour, baking powder and cheese in a large bowl. In a separate bowl, mix the milk and egg together, then slowly pour into the flour mixture and beat with a handheld electric whisk until all the ingredients are well mixed.

Stir in the onion, mushrooms and chopped ham with a wooden spoon until evenly dispersed.

Spoon the mixture into the paper cases until two-thirds full and bake in the preheated oven for 30–35 minutes, or until deep golden and the sponge bounces back when touched. A skewer inserted in the centre should come out clean. Leave the muffins to cool slightly in the tray before turning out onto a wire cooling rack to cool completely.

## carrot and courgette muffins

**Some people are surprised to hear that courgettes can be used in muffins, but they work well and give these muffins added colour.**

2 eggs
200 g soft light brown sugar
80 ml sunflower oil
260 g plain flour
2 teaspoons baking powder
2 teaspoons ground cinnamon
80 ml natural yoghurt
½ teaspoon vanilla extract
120 g shelled walnuts, chopped
250 g carrots, grated
120 g courgette, grated

*a 12-hole muffin tray, lined with paper cases*

**Makes 12**

Preheat the oven to 170°C (325°F) Gas 3.

Put the eggs, sugar and oil in an electric mixer with a paddle attachment (or use a handheld electric whisk) and beat on slow speed until well combined. In a separate bowl, sift together the flour, baking powder and cinnamon, then add to the egg mixture. Beat until everything is well incorporated.

Add the yoghurt and vanilla extract and mix through until well combined. Stir in the walnuts, carrots and courgette with a wooden spoon until evenly dispersed.

Spoon the mixture into the paper cases until two-thirds full and bake in the preheated oven for 25–30 minutes, or until deep golden and the sponge bounces back when touched. A skewer inserted in the centre should come out clean. Leave the muffins to cool slightly in the tray before turning out onto a wire cooling rack to cool completely.

# spinach and cheese muffins

Here's another delicious savoury muffin that is always popular at the Bakery. Most types of hard cheese can be used, so feel free to try different varieties.

30 g butter

½ small red onion, finely chopped

360 g plain flour

2½ teaspoons baking powder

1 teaspoon cayenne pepper

250 g Cheddar cheese, grated

220 ml whole milk

1 egg

130 g baby spinach leaves

*a 12-hole muffin tray, lined with paper cases*

**Makes 12**

Preheat the oven to 170°C (325°F) Gas 3.

Melt the butter in a saucepan over medium heat, then fry the onion until cooked. Set aside.

Put the flour, baking powder, cayenne and cheese in a large bowl. In a separate bowl, mix the milk and egg together, then slowly pour into the flour mixture and beat with a handheld electric whisk until all the ingredients are well mixed.

Stir in the onion and spinach with a wooden spoon until evenly dispersed.

Spoon the mixture into the paper cases until two-thirds full and bake in the preheated oven for 30–35 minutes, or until deep golden and the sponge bounces back when touched. A skewer inserted in the centre should come out clean. Leave the muffins to cool slightly in the tray before turning out onto a wire cooling rack to cool completely.

# chocolate muffins

**You can vary this recipe by adding dark, milk or white chocolate chips.**

2 eggs
200 g caster sugar
130 g plain flour
50 g cocoa powder
2 teaspoons baking powder
a pinch of salt
160 ml whole milk
¼ teaspoon vanilla extract
160 g unsalted butter, melted
120 g dark chocolate, roughly chopped

*a 12-hole muffin tray, lined with paper cases*

**Makes 12**

Preheat the oven to 170°C (325°F) Gas 3.

Put the eggs and sugar in a freestanding electric mixer with a paddle attachment (or use a handheld electric whisk) and beat until pale and well combined.

In a separate bowl, sift together the flour, cocoa powder, baking powder and salt. In another bowl, combine the milk and vanilla extract. Gradually beat these 2 mixtures alternately into the egg mixture little by little (scrape any unmixed ingredients from the side of the bowl with a rubber spatula). Beat until all the ingredients are well incorporated.

Stir in the melted butter with a wooden spoon until well incorporated, then stir in the chocolate until evenly dispersed.

Spoon the mixture into the paper cases until two-thirds full and bake in the preheated oven for about 30 minutes, or until the sponge bounces back when touched. A skewer inserted in the centre should come out clean. Leave the muffins to cool slightly in the tray before turning out onto a wire cooling rack to cool completely.

# blueberry muffins

**The classic muffin – and the perfect start to the day with a cup of strong tea.**

360 g plain flour
370 g caster sugar
1 teaspoon salt
1½ teaspoons baking powder
½ teaspoon bicarbonate of soda
375 ml buttermilk
1 egg
½ teaspoon vanilla extract
70 g unsalted butter, melted
250 g blueberries

*a 12-hole muffin tray, lined with paper cases*

**Makes 12**

Preheat the oven to 170°C (325°F) Gas 3.

Put the flour, sugar, salt, baking powder and bicarbonate of soda in a freestanding electric mixer with a paddle attachment (or use a handheld electric whisk) and beat on slow speed.

Put the buttermilk, egg and vanilla extract into a jug and mix to combine. Slowly pour into the flour mixture and beat until all the ingredients are incorporated.

Pour in the melted butter and beat until the butter has just been incorporated, then turn the mixer up to medium speed and beat until the dough is even and smooth.

Finally, gently fold in the blueberries with a wooden spoon until evenly dispersed.

Spoon the mixture into the paper cases until two-thirds full and bake in the preheated oven for 20–25 minutes, or until golden brown and the sponge bounces back when touched. A skewer inserted in the centre should come out clean. Leave the muffins to cool slightly in the tray before turning out onto a wire cooling rack to cool completely.

# banana and cinnamon muffins

**Moist and sweet, nuts or chocolate chips can be added for variety.**

350 g plain flour

¾ teaspoon salt

1½ teaspoons baking powder

½ teaspoon bicarbonate of soda

2 teaspoons ground cinnamon, plus extra to sprinkle

160 g caster sugar, plus extra to sprinkle

375 ml buttermilk

1 egg

½ teaspoon vanilla extract

70 g unsalted butter, melted

400 g peeled banana, mashed

*a 12-hole muffin tray, lined with paper cases*

**Makes 12**

Preheat the oven to 170°C (325°F) Gas 3.

Put the flour, sugar, salt, baking powder, bicarbonate of soda and cinnamon in a large bowl and beat with a handheld electric whisk until combined.

Put the buttermilk, egg and vanilla extract in a jug and mix to combine. Slowly pour into the flour mixture and beat on slow speed until all the ingredients are incorporated.

Pour in the melted butter and beat until incorporated. Stir in the bananas with a wooden spoon until evenly dispersed.

Spoon the mixture into the paper cases until two-thirds full and sprinkle a little extra sugar and cinnamon over the tops. Bake in the preheated oven for 20–30 minutes, or until golden brown and the sponge bounces back when touched. A skewer inserted in the centre should come out clean. Leave the muffins to cool slightly in the tray before turning out onto a wire cooling rack to cool completely.

# maple and pecan muffins

**Maple syrup and pecan nuts are a classic combination, with the syrup helping to make the muffins irresistibly moist and sweet.**

350 g plain flour

160 g caster sugar

¾ teaspoon salt

1½ teaspoons baking powder

½ teaspoon bicarbonate of soda

375 ml buttermilk

1 egg

½ teaspoon vanilla extract

70 g unsalted butter, melted

240 g shelled pecan nuts, chopped, plus 12 pecan halves to decorate

200 ml maple syrup

*a 12-hole muffin tray, lined with paper cases*

**Makes 12**

Preheat the oven to 170°C (325°F) Gas 3.

Put the flour, sugar, salt, baking powder and bicarbonate of soda in a large bowl and beat with a handheld electric whisk until combined.

Put the buttermilk, egg and vanilla extract in a jug and mix to combine. Slowly pour into the flour mixture and beat on slow speed until all the ingredients are incorporated.

Pour in the melted butter and beat until incorporated. Stir in 100 ml of the maple syrup and the pecan nuts with a wooden spoon until evenly dispersed.

Spoon the mixture into the paper cases until two-thirds full and drizzle the remaining maple syrup over the tops. Finish with a pecan half in the centre of each one. Bake in the preheated oven for 20–30 minutes, or until golden brown and the sponge bounces back when touched. A skewer inserted in the centre should come out clean. Leave the muffins to cool slightly in the tray before turning out onto a wire cooling rack to cool completely.

# cookies